Hitler and the Collapse of Weimar Germany

D0947567

Martin Broszat

Hitler
and the Collapse of
Weimar Germany

Translated and with a Foreword by
V. R. Berghahn

BERG
Leamington Spa / Hamburg / New York

Berg Publishers Limited
24 Binswood Avenue, Leamington Spa, CV32 5SQ, UK
Schenefelder Landstr. 14K, 2000 Hamburg 55, W.-Germany
175 Fifth Avenue/Room 400, New York, NY 10010, USA

© Berg Publishers 1987
Reprinted 1989

First published in 1984 as *Die Machtergreifung.*
Der Aufstieg der NSDAP und die Zerstörung der Weimarer
Republik, by Deutscher Taschenbuch Verlag, Munich
© Deutscher Taschenbuch Verlag GmbH & Co. KG, Munich

Distributed exclusively in the US and Canada by
St. Martin's Press, New York

British Library Cataloguing in Publication Data

Broszat, Martin
    Hitler and the collapse of Weimar Germany.
    1. Germany—Politics and government—
    1918–1933
    I. Title   II. Die Machtergreifung. *English*
    943.085   DD256.5

    ISBN 0–85496–509–2
    ISBN 0–85496–517–3 Pbk

**Library of Congress Cataloging-in-Publication
Data**

Broszat, Martin.
    Hitler and the collapse of Weimar Germany.

    Translation of: Die Machtergreifung.
    Bibliography: p.
    Includes index.
    1. Germany—Politics and government—1918–1933.
    2. Nationalsozialistische Deutsche Arbeiter-Partei—
    History. I. Title.
    DD240.B81513 1987 943.085   86–26857
    ISBN 0–85496–509–2
    ISBN 0–85496–517–3 (pbk.)

Printed in Great Britain by Billings of Worcester

Contents

Foreword   *V. R. Berghahn*   vii

Introduction Hitler and the Nazi Party in Munich,
   1919–1923/4   1

1. Berlin in the Autumn of 1930   11
   1.1. Economic Crisis and Political Radicalisation   11
   1.2. Goebbel's Struggle for Berlin: Methods, Crises,
        Contradictions   18
   1.3. The Prussian Government and Police as the Main
        Opponents   25
   1.4. The Boycott of Remarque's Film *All Quiet on the
        Western Front*   32

2. National Socialism and the Weimar Republic   37
   2.1. The Historical Preconditions of National
        Socialism   37
   2.2. Hitler and the NSDAP during the Period of
        Stabilisation, 1924–1928   50
   2.3. The Nazi Party as a Mass Movement in the Political
        and Economic Crisis of 1929–1933   67

3. The Process of the Nazi Assumption of Power   93
   3.1. The Brüning Era   94
   3.2. The Final Phase and the Destruction of the Republic
        under Papen   115

4. The Final Stages of Hitler's Rise to the Chancellorship 129
   4.1. The Meeting of 4 January 1933   129
   4.2. The Mobilisation of the Reichslandbund   135
   4.3. Hectic Activity at Ribbentrop's House   138
   4.4. The Removal of Last-Minute Qualms   142
   4.5. Postscript   146

Select Bibliography   151

Index of Names   155

Foreword

Martin Broszat is undoubtedly to be ranked as one of the foremost of the many historians of the Nazi period. Over the past thirty years or so he has published half a dozen books and innumerable articles on this subject. As director of the well-known *Institut für Zeitgeschichte* at Munich he has encouraged and promoted research by others into this most depressing, confusing and crucial period of modern German and European history. His own work ranges from studies on Nazi occupation policy in Poland to a structural analysis of the Hitler regime. He has made important contributions to the debate between the 'intentionalists' and 'functionalists' concerning the centrality of Hitler to the evolution of the Third Reich. Most recently he has extended his work into the 'grass-roots' of German society and has become an advocate of popular history in the Anglo-Saxon tradition which tries to reconstruct the experiences of ordinary people. Given the importance of his work, it is regrettable that only one of his books, *The Hitler State*, has so far appeared in translation. The publication of this work is an attempt to rectify this and to enable an English-speaking readership to share Professor Broszat's sophisticated insights into the nature of Nazism which he gained through his long study of the subject.

However, this is not the only purpose behind translating this book. As far as I can see, there are many monographs and even more survey-type studies on the *early* Weimar Republic. There are also a number of general analyses dealing with the Third Reich, as it were, in action. But the reader who is interested in an up-to-date account of the rise·of Nazism and the collapse of the Weimar Republic will have to turn to one of the collections of essays which came out in 1983 on the occasion of the fiftieth anniversary of Hitler's seizure of power. Such anthologies inevitably leave gaps and lack in the cohesion which one author can give to his or her comprehensive examination of the subject.

Having taught the history of interwar Germany at British universities for many years, I have certainly been looking for a short study which one could ask students to read for next week's class to be devoted to the complexities of the collapse of the Weimar Republic. The virtue of Professor Broszat's book is not only that his is such a study, but also that it deliberately moves away from the high-level structural analyses, so typical of much of modern German scholarship, which become intelligible only after one has read every sentence twice. Thus he would probably be the first to admit that *The Hitler State* does not exactly make easy reading. This book takes a different stylistic approach and does not expect the reader to have a profound knowledge of the period. It is written with a good eye for the telling quotation and illustration which succeeds in holding the reader's attention and permits things to fall into place. At the same time the authority which he can bring to bear is never lost and at no point does the book therefore lapse into shallow narrative.

Professor Broszat sets the stage in two introductory sections; the first one is concerned with the early origins and character of the Nazi movement *in Munich* up to the crisis of 1923 and the failed coup of November of that year. The second introductory section looks at another major crisis of the Weimar Republic and, like the first one, provides a fascinating account of the situation *in Berlin* in 1930–1, indicating that the Nazis had by now moved well beyond the confines of Bavarian politics. The use of eye-witness material and contemporary newspaper reports adds to the liveliness and readability of this section. Against the background of these two 'curtain-raisers', the author moves back in time and thenceforth begins to provide his systematic and controlled analysis of 'Hitler and the Collapse of the Weimar Republic'. A good deal of attention is being paid here to the growth of the Nazi movement; but this account is always embedded in the larger context of the socio-economic and political development of Germany as a whole.

It is only towards the end of the book that Professor Broszat deliberately narrows his focus again to the politics of intrigue and manoeuvering in the immediate run-up to Hitler's nomination as Reich Chancellor on 30 January 1933. However, in his meticulous pursuit of these events, he does not mean to imply that he proposes to reduce the Nazi seizure of power to last-minute twists and turns and to a series of unforeseen and unforeseeable accidents. Rather he emphasises even now the broader framework of the structural preconditions of the January 1933 outcome and of the ideological and social–psychological affinities which brought the conservative elites and the Hitler movement together in their joint endeavour to destroy the parliamentary Republic of Weimar which they all so hated — with consequences and costs that shape Germany, Europe and, indeed, the rest of the world to this day. Given this centrality of the period of German history covered by this book to an understanding of subsequent events up to the Second World War and beyond, Professor Broszat's concise study is to be welcomed. I hope that readers will find it as instructive as I have found it.

V.R. BERGHAHN

Introduction
Hitler and the Nazi Party in Munich
1919–1923/4

Between May 1919, after the short-lived Soviet Republic had been destroyed by Free Corps units, and November 1923, when the so-called Hitler Putsch was quelled, Munich, the capital for Bavaria, became a haven for Bavarian separatists and *völkische* nationalists who were fundamentally opposed to the Weimar Republic which had emerged from the defeat of Germany in the First World War and the Revolution of 1918–19. This opposition rejected the centralism and republicanism of Berlin and nourished in its wake a militant paramilitarism as well as a small anti-Semitic party which, starting from even more modest beginnings, had renamed itself National Socialist German Workers' Party (NSDAP) in February 1920. In September 1919, while it still operated under the name of German Workers' Party (DAP), this splinter group had been joined by a thirty-year-old man who, within a short period, subordinated it to him. This man was Adolf Hitler. A few years later, in 1922–3, some people would call him 'King of Munich'. Hitler, a failed student of architecture from Austria and former front-line soldier in the First World War, started his political career in Munich as an agitator in the counter-revolutionary hothouse atmosphere after the collapse of the Bavarian Soviet Republic. Here, in the depressed situation following the German defeat and revolution, he could generalise and politicise his feelings of personal bitterness and hatred which were rooted in his own failure and his rejection of the unpleasant realities of life and which had led him, already as an adolescent, to develop fantastic plans for the future and to evade regular employment. This background helps to explain his passionate hatred against what he saw as the source of all evil: 'Jewish' pacifism and internationalism. He also fervently proclaimed the only remedy against these evils. The task was to fight them determinedly and to make Germany great again.

1

These slogans formed the core of the rhetoric which Hitler developed and began to master, as he travelled from rally to rally in the early 1920s.

The suggestive power which he radiated and the persuasiveness of his hard-hitting language have been confirmed by many of his listeners. He looked like an ordinary man, still youngish and mostly pale-faced. A strain of his dark hair fell across his forehead. His posture was tensely erect with his head thrown backwards. He underlined his radical verbal attacks by rhythmically pushing his outstretched index finger forward. A moment later Hitler would resort to expansive gestures when, like a missionary and in a baritone voice, he spoke about his visions of the future. The themes of speeches which he was making in 1920 in Munich beer halls by their dozens were the same: the 'shame of the Versailles Treaty', the enemies within who had stabbed the nation in the back, the problem of 'might and right', of 'workers and the nation', and, invariably, the 'Jewish Question'. What marked him out among the speakers of the political Right in Munich was the *way* in which he put his message across.

Early verdicts on his style were: a 'born popular orator', 'masterly' or 'extremely skilful'. Above all, he knew how to stimulate his audiences and to keep them hanging on his words, often for two or three hours, by resorting to biting sarcasm. He ridiculed his opponents as 'liars' or spoke of the 'miserable weaklings' in the government and in other political parties. Police reports almost always noted that there was 'lively applause', 'tempestuous applause' or 'long-lasting applause' at the end of his appearances. Hitler resorted to verbal attacks and preached hatred. And yet the anti-Nazi press stated no more than half the truth when it dubbed him an 'extremely cunning demagogue' or 'leader of an anti-Semitic' party. His greatest talent as a demagogue was that he knew how to wrap his constant call to fight the 'parasites' and 'enemies of the people' in a solemn appeal to show national pride and to believe in Germany's strength which he presented in deep earnestness. He could talk of the rebirth of the nation in a tone of religious conviction which almost always guaranteed him a profoundly moved audience.

Soon Hitler, the 'drummer', had become indispensable as a

magnet of this kind. Even before asserting his dictatorial leadership of the party in July 1921, he pushed his comrades on the executive into organising one propaganda campaign after the other; for to be successful and to gain power was synonymous at this time above all with drawing attention to oneself and with attracting the masses. As early as February 1921 Hitler could risk renting the large *Zirkus Krone* assembly hall for a mass rally of the NSDAP. New propaganda techniques which had been developed first and foremost by Hitler assumed great significance. There were the glaring red colours of the swastika flag which had been adopted by the Party in 1920; there were aggressive posters and announcements of rallies. Leaflets were distributed from lorries which were driven around town. Assembly hall protection was put in the hands of young brawlers who wore swastika armbands and were soon to become members of the SA Brownshirts. From 1921 these contingents appeared in closed formations headed by a marching band and provided the radical Hitler movement with an image of military discipline and order.

Hitler's messianic power and dynamism also drove wealthy supporters and patrons into his arms who made a vital contribution to furnishing Hitler's often airy-fairy exuberance with a few solid institutional and social struts. One of them was (and remained until the coup of November 1923) Captain Ernst Röhm, a staff-officer with the local *Reichswehr* command in Munich. Röhm had considerable gifts as an organiser and was a swashbuckling activist on the nationalist Right. He could be found pulling all kinds of wires whenever it was a matter of undermining the disarmament clauses of the Versailles Treaty. Thus he could be seen organising local militias (*Einwohnerwehren*) or caches of arms. He also helped to equip the Free Corps and the militant Patriotic Leagues (VVVD). From the start Röhm saw in Hitler a propagandistic genius of the *völkische* movement and supported him wherever possible. Hitler also had much reason to be grateful, in those early days, to a man very different from Röhm. He was Dietrich Eckart, a völkisch and anti-Semitic poet and journalist. In 1920 Eckart was instrumental in helping the Nazis to acquire the *Völkischer Beobachter*, whose editor he remained until his death in 1923. Eckart was well-educated and quite wealthy. He also had many connections with the academic and *haut bourgeois* establishment of Munich. He, like many other *völkische* romantics after him, particularly admired Hitler's magnetic power over the masses and his robust and brutal energy. He was among the first to encourage, as a 'paternal friend', Hitler in his leadership ambitions. He polished Hitler's prose and opened many doors for him among like-minded people in Munich's high society.

Finally, the patronage of Ernst Pöhner, the president of the Munich police, was particularly valuable to Hitler in this early period. He was assisted by Dr Wilhelm Frick who was in charge of the political department, and both of them saw to it that the inflammatory and violent activities of the NSDAP and the SA were invariably covered up and that embarrassing investigations by the police or the judiciary were blocked.

One thing had meanwhile become abundantly clear, Hitler's image as a propagandist was only one side of the coin. The title 'King of Munich' also implied something else: the sarcastic, half-approving or cynical support for the questionable methods with which Hitler had turned himself into an overlord of Munich's squares and assembly halls. He was the 'King' of a political banditry which he had done much to proliferate. Hitler, the *Führer*, was at the same time the Chieftain (*Anführer*) of the provocations and brutalities which the Nazis and the SA engaged in. Thus he was in charge when on 9 August 1921 a rally of the *Bayernbund* was broken up and Otto Ballerstedt, who had long been an irritant to the NSDAP, was hauled down from the rostrum. In November of that year Hitler signalled the start of a brawl in the Munich *Hofbräuhaus* in which dozens of Social Democrats were beaten up. One of the most brutal street fights occurred at Coburg in the middle of October 1922, with Hitler, supported by the bourgeois press, claiming a major victory over the 'Reds'.

Provocative brutalities, especially if directed against the 'Socialists', had a deterrent effect, but were also designed to command the respect of the middle classes of Coburg and other places. Hitler was quick to recognise this. He also promoted the image of being the domineering leader of a paramilitary association who would run about with a dog-whip and a pistol and made his appearance in a fast sports car. He surrounded himself with 'buddies' and bodyguards — types like Emil Maurice,

Hermann Esser, Ulrich Graf and Christian Weber. He saw himself confirmed in his approach to politics by the fact that his antics gained the respect of sympathetic circles in Munich's high society, especially among the Bechsteins, Bruckmanns and Hanfstaengls. His reputation was that of a political *enfant terrible* who succeeded in arousing an almost morbid interest in himself and in evincing maternal–erotic feelings of affection among some of the ladies of Munich's salon culture. According to eye-witnesses Hitler, when moving in this milieu, changed into a modest, shy and often almost clumsy man who relaxed only once he had started to pontificate about Richard Wagner, the Jews or politics in general.

These contacts enabled him to gain personal esteem and a position which was independent of his party commitment. It also opened up new sources of finance. That Hitler had long left the unassuming circle of a *völkisch* sectarianism is evidenced by the fact that in 1922 he was joined by Hermann Göring who took charge of the SA in the following year. Göring was the last commander of the famous Richthofen Air Squadron. He came from a family of higher civil servants in the Imperial period and was married to an elegant Swedish woman. As the *Wiener Presse* put it in 1923, Hitler had become the 'dominant figure of the nationalist movement in South Germany', although by this time his reputation had spread beyond the frontiers of Bavaria and the Ruhr industrialist Emil Kirdorf had become captivated by him. Finally there was the main hero of the nationalist camp, General Erich Ludendorff, who had moved to Munich in 1920 and who from 1922 onwards appeared side by side with Hitler.

Meanwhile the SA had grown out of its early role as a protection squad of Nazi rallies. Increasingly it had turned itself into a paramilitary group which, though loyal to Hitler personally, operated independently of the NSDAP. This development had the advantage that the SA, like other paramilitary associations, was able to enjoy the aid in weapons and training provided by the Bavarian *Reichswehr*. The disadvantage from Hitler's point of view was that he was forced to co-operate with other associations more than he would have liked to. There was also the problem that the military leadership of the SA, together with those leagues which linked up with it in 1923, gained a weight of its own that undermined Hitler's position as sole leader. Nevertheless, he succeeded in building up, with the support of the militant SA and its affiliates, not just a political power position, but also a revolutionary potential of some military significance.

The ups and downs in Hitler's political opportunities in Munich depended to a large extent on the degree of tension between the central government in Berlin and the Bavarian government; there was also the varying acuteness of anti-Berlin sentiments which began to harden among the Bavarian establishment as a result of these tensions between 1919 and 1923.

The forces of nationalism and counter-revolution in Bavaria received a first boost after the failure of the Kapp Putsch against the Berlin government in March 1920. Whereas the so-called Weimar Coalition, consisting of Social Democrats, Left Liberals and the Catholic Centre Party, was reconstituted at the centre, an openly counter-revolutionary, conservative–nationalist government was formed in Munich. Gustav von Kahr, the regional administrator for Upper Bavaria, was elected Minister President, notably because he had enhanced his reputation as a persistent promoter of the Bavarian militia movement. By 1920 these *Einwohnerwehren* had grown to some 300,000 men, thus making a mockery of the disarmament clauses of the Versailles Treaty. Hermann Kriebel, the chief of staff of these organisations and their illegal successors was to be a major figure in the events of 8–9 November 1923. At the insistence of the Allies the Reich government had demanded the dissolution of the *Einwohnerwehren*. Kahr's resistance to this in 1920–1 had turned him into a kind of protector of all anti-republican and counter-revolutionary forces who had begun to congregate in Bavaria during the early 1920s and who saw in him a standard-bearer of their political hopes and expectations. However, his policy of resistance became ultimately untenable. In September 1921 he was forced to resign. There followed a one-year spell under a more moderate government led by Hugo Count von Lerchenfeld during which the Nazi Party also had to operate in a less clement political climate. Pöhner and Frick were transferred to other duties. At one point in the spring of 1922 the Bavarian government even seriously considered the deportation of Hitler, who was an Austrian citizen. The leader of the Nazi movement hence had to reckon with the worst. However, in July and August 1922, following the ratification of the Law for the Protection of the Republic, renewed conflict broke out between Bavaria and the central government. Protest rallies were held in Munich against 'Jew-pervaded Berlin'. These events together with rapidly escalating inflation provided Hitler with a fresh opportunity. A mass demonstration which the Bavarian 'Block of Order' had called demonstrated that he was far from commanding a majority among the patriotic bourgeoisie of Munich; but Hitler did succeed in presenting his movement as the vanguard of a nationalist activism. Given the broad groundswell of anti-republican protest, his extremist agitation and the appearance of his SA contingents proved once more very effective. Julius Streicher, the leader of a strong grouping in Nuremberg and Franconia, was so impressed that he subordinated himself to the leader of the NSDAP whose membership rose to 50,000 by the autumn of 1923.

As early as the autumn of 1922 Hitler and other leaders of the radical associations spoke up in favour of a return of Kahr. He was to be endowed with dictatorial powers and the associations expected to gain a tangible share in the decision-making. But this solution had to wait. There was instead the interlude of the government of Engen von Knilling, a sort of compromise solution between Lerchenfeld and Kahr. Hitler responded with a fresh wave of demonstrations. There was talk of dictatorship and of the need for taking action. By the beginning of 1923 such demands became more and more frantic.

The notion that actual fighting was required rather than passive resistance prepared the ground for the formation of a block of radical paramilitary groups close to Hitler in the spring of 1923 which, led militarily by Kriebel, was to become the centre of activism on 8–9 November when the so-called Hitler Putsch occurred.

While up to the summer of 1923 Hitler suffered a number of defeats at the hands of the Bavarian authorities and especially a trial of strength between the paramilitary associations and the Knilling Cabinet on 1 May turned into a fiasco for the *Führer*, developments at the national level worked in his favour. Faced with galloping inflation the new Reich government of Gustav Stresemann in September 1923 called off the passive resistance against the French occupation of the Ruhr area which had taken place in January 1923 as a means of enforcing reparations deliveries. By the autumn political thunder-storms were also gathering over Bavaria. To deal with the escalating crisis Kahr was recalled as the embodiment of Bavarian independence and nationalism. He was nominated *Generalstaatskommissar* and equipped with far-reaching powers. Meanwhile Stresemann tried to develop a rational policy to deal with the crisis. But his strategy was denounced as a 'policy of fulfillment' of Allied demands and the anti-Berlin sentiments among the Patriotic Associations, and hence also Hitler's NSDAP, received a tremendous fillip. The Bavarian government became particularly worried when, on 1/2 September at a rally in Nuremberg Hitler had appeared next to Ludendorff and when calls for a Hitler–Ludendorff dictatorship could be heard. The danger posed by the Patriotic Leagues, which the government had pampered for several years, was suddenly thrown into sharp relief: in an atmosphere of heightened excitement it was quite possible that they would join the radicals around Hitler and Kriebel. That this was beginning to happen, is evidenced by the behaviour of the *Oberland* League, led by Friedrich Weber, and the *Reichsflagge* under Friedrich Heiss. On 25 September both organisations put themselves at the disposal of the Hitler grouping.

The nomination of Kahr was therefore designed to counter the drift into radicalism in view of the fact that he enjoyed a high reputation among the nationalists. But he had been in office for no more than a few days when he willy-nilly contributed to an intensification of the crisis. At the end of September Otto Geßler, the *Reichswehr* Minister in the Berlin Cabinet, demanded a ban on the *Völkischer Beobachter*. The Nazi paper was charged with having published an inflammatory article against Stresemann and Hans von Seeckt, the Army Chief. Kahr and Otto von Lossow, the Bavarian *Reichswehr* commander, resisted this demand. They wished to avoid a clash with the Nazis and the other Bavarian nationalist associations. When Geßler thereupon dismissed Lossow, the latter having obtained Kahr's backing, refused to comply. Instead he made the Bavarian *Reichswehr* contingents take an oath to him as their commander. In fact this was a breach of the constitution, even if Kahr and Lossow merely intended it to be a threat which was not to be taken seriously. Hitler, on the other hand, thought that the moment had now come for him to persuade the authoritarian Bavarian government to secede from the Reich. This, he hoped, would provide him with the opportunity to put himself and the associations led by him at the head of the march on Berlin. He clearly misjudged the situation, but his assessment formed the background to the attempted coup of 8/9 November 1923.

The events at the Munich *Bürgerbräukeller* in the evening of 8 November, which in some ways assumed the proportions of a soap opera, have been related in a number of other studies. It is also well-known how Kahr and Lossow who had been bullied in the *Bürgerbräukeller* encounter into supporting a march on Berlin on the following morning changed their minds during the night. When Hitler, Ludendorff and their followers assembled in the centre of Munich on the morning of the 9 November to start a 'national revolution' with the support of the Bavarian authorities, they faced strong police contingents with machine-guns trying to block their way. Suddenly shots were fired, most probably at first by the heavily armed marchers. The police responded and there followed pandemonium. Hitler and his troops panicked and then took to their heels. Only Ludendorff marched on and was soon arrested. Hitler's arrest came two days later at the house of his friend 'Putzi' Hanfstaengl where he had taken refuge. He was taken to Landsberg prison. All in all the Bavarian police took some 216 persons into custody in connection with the putsch. The trial against the mass defendants, the so-called *Hitler-Prozeß*, opened on 26 February and ended on 1 April 1924. Hitler was sentenced to five years, but was released on probation before Christmas 1924. Without delay he started to rebuild his party. Although the November Putsch had failed miserably, the experience had also taught Hitler certain lessons which he began to apply from 1925 onwards and which we shall have to come back to in a later chapter after an examination of Nazi politics at the time of another major crisis in Weimar history in 1930–1.

1
Berlin in the Autumn of 1930

1.1. *Economic Crisis and Political Radicalisation*

The number of unemployed had been increased by further redundancies of workers and white-collar employees at Siemens, Borsig, Berliner Verkehrs-A.G. and many small- and medium-sized firms.[1] On 15 November 1930, even before the beginning of the winter, every tenth person out of some 2.5 million employed in a total population for Greater Berlin of 4.3 million was without a job. A mere two-thirds of them received small amounts of unemployment benefit or special crisis payments; the rest were forced to live on meagre benefits provided by community welfare schemes, if they were not left without any support.

Some 64 per cent of all male unemployed in the Reich capital belonged to the age groups below 30. The worst hit were the 14 to 18-year-olds who had just left school. Almost 20 per cent of all unemployed were in these cohorts. But also those with academic qualifications mostly found the doors closed to them. Graduates of the Technical University at Berlin–Charlottenburg who had been trained as engineers and architects failed to find appropriate employment and had to accept positions as 'technicians' lower down the salary scale. The professions — doctors and lawyers — had too many qualified people. There was little difference between the monthly income of a skilled worker (ca. 200 marks) and that of the majority of the doctors in Berlin who relied on social insurance patients. The Health Service (*Krankenkasse*) paid on average a mere 80 pfennigs per patient requiring treatment.

The department stores in the city had succeeded in maintaining their turnover at the previous year's level by slashing their

1. Many details of this section are based on an evaluation of the Berlin press for the second half of 1930, in particular *Vossische Zeitung, Berliner Tageblatt, Der Jungdeutsche* and *Illustrierte Republikanische Zeitung*.

prices dramatically. Thus the Wertheim Stores offered fashionable ladies' dresses and ball gowns for as little as 20 marks. But meanwhile the decline in prices and demand had ruined innumerable corner shops, craftsmen and small industrial enterprises. In the economics pages of the *Vossische Zeitung* appeared within one week at the beginning of November announcements of no less than nine bankruptcies of local firms: Ernst (a shoemaker), the Voigt paper factory, the draperies shop of Wassermann, the Krause furniture factory, the interior architect Schwarzschild, the electrics workshop of Frank & Co., the building firm of Hartje, the soap manufacturers of Krefft & Arndt and Zellermayer, the delicatessen.

Meat consumption declined by four per cent in comparison with 1929 and the price of a pound of pork had risen to 1.20 marks. Car production slumped by 35 per cent. There were 20,000 people in the Reich in 1930 who bought a new car, but there were twice as many who wanted to sell their car. Public construction was still going encouragingly strong and the suburban commuter network was being extended along Frankfurter Allee to Neukölln, Tempelhof and Pankow; slum clearing continued in the Wedding district and buildings were being added to the University. Above all the Berlin council housing programme promoted by the *Berliner Wohnungsfürsorgegesellschaft* reached a new peak. In 1930 some 37,000 low-cost flats were completed as against ca. 20,000 in previous years. But budget deficits forced the local council to cut these programmes considerably for 1931. Flats in older properties, expensive shops and offices in the city centre and luxury houses in Wannsee, Babelsberg and Grunewald were being sold or auctioned off at knock-down prices because the owners were unable to find tenants or to pay their mortgages.

On the Berlin stock market, shares of the I.G. Farben chemicals trust dropped from 187 to 129 points in the second half of 1930, those of the AEG electrical engineering firm from 169 to 100. Meanwhile the press reported extensively about the outcome of the trials in Hamburg-Altona against the Schleswig-Holstein bombers. At the beginning of November another trial started at Königsberg against radicals in the agrarian *Landvolk* movement. The origins of these trials were invariably the same: peasant demonstrations and riots which had been triggered by compulsory auctions of farms and the impounding of animals and agricultural machinery. In 1930 some 25,000 hectares of farmland were sold at compulsory auctions in East Prussia alone.

In the middle of October a strike was called by some 140,000 metal workers in Berlin, who decided to resist proposed wage cuts. The strike lasted for two weeks. As the *Vossische Zeitung* reported on 18 October 1930:

> Siemensstadt, Wedding, Reinickendorf, Eichbaumstrasse, Tegel — the factory chimney-stacks point into the blue autumn skies. Menacing, cooled down, petrified. There is quiet in the factory yards; the wheels have been halted. There is the long road stretching from the factory gates. Groups of workers are standing ten yards apart, wearing cardigans under their cloth jackets, blue caps with a badge, smoking a pipe. The district has taken the days off, but it is a time of bitterness. There is no smile on the faces; they look worn, embittered. There are discussions; the size of the groups grows; speeches become more heated. The big factory gate is locked. A rope demarcates a restricted access area; two red flags. Police are on patrol duty. In one of the local pubs [we see] the strike leadership behind a long table. One worker after another steps forward with his yellow strike-card. They collect their strike pay every day — twenty marks per week for an unmarried person. . . . The problem cases are presented by those who are not unionised, but are also out of work.

Ultimately the strike was unsuccessful. In November the majority of the unionised workforce voted to accept the decision of an arbitrator who had proposed a 6 per cent wage-cut.

There was an increasingly sharper contrast between the growing poverty of workers, white-collar employees and small self-employed and the conspicuous wealth, the elegant fashions, the glamorous facades of amusement arcades or splendid press balls with well-known artists, writers and sportsmen which could be seen in the west end of Berlin around the main boulevard of *Kurfürstendamm*. Since the beginning of the crisis a number of avant-garde pieces of social criticism had been taken off the screens and stages of the city. Instead and next to classical plays there had been a revival of operettas, floor shows and sentimental love films. The six-day bicycle races at the *Berliner Radrennbahn* also enjoyed increased popularity. The *Deutsches Theater* put on a new production by Max Reinhardt of Shakespeare's *Midsummer Night's Dream*. The *Schiller Theater* showed Jürgen Fehling's production of *Nora*; the *Ufa* Cinema Palace near the Zoo Station around the corner from *Kurfürstendamm* ran Ernst Lubitsch's *Love Parade*, an operetta spectacle. Meanwhile the *Volksbühne* (subscription theatre) witnessed a decline in its membership, whereas technically well-produced entertainment movies attracted larger and larger audiences. The success of *The Blue Angel* with Marlene Dietrich and Emil Jannings was surpassed only by the sentimental film *Favourite of the Gods*. Although *Ufa* (Universal Film Ltd) had made large investments in sound equipment for its studios and cinemas, the company ended the year without losses.

The plight of artists and the self-employed must also be seen against the background of a partisan protectionism. Although the higher administrative court subsequently largely exonerated him, it was this protectionism which led to the downfall of the Mayor Otto Böss in November 1930. Swift justice magistrates courts were instituted in the Alexanderplatz police HQ in an attempt to deal with increased petty crime. It took one and a half hours to deal with three cases: an elderly unemployed man who, in passing a fruit stand, had snatched two apples, was acquitted; a chambermaid in a Berlin hotel who had hidden three towels under her skirt, was fined twenty marks; a Communist and journeyman saddler was locked up for three days for abusing a policeman and resisting arrest. Most of the serious cases involving political crimes and violent demonstrations came before the Moabit High Court, and there was a growing number of these cases instigated either by Communists or National Socialists.

The forces of the Berlin police president Zörgiebel, decried as 'Zörgiebel Cossacks' by the Communists or as 'bloodhounds' by the Nazis, established a tough regime when they searched for weapons and launched truncheon assaults. They were quick to arrest people when it was a matter of controlling suspicious assemblies and demonstrations with lorry convoys or when they moved in to dissolve assembly hall brawls or street fights between Communists and Nazis. However, it proved impossible to prevent violence and the perpetrators and motives of many cases were never identified. Thus the police were without a clue in the case of the unemployed SA man Ganzert who was found on 30 September in his Charlottenburg with a fatal gun wound after he had been involved in a late-evening incident in the regular drinking place of the local Brownshirt detachment. And the judges of the magistrates court of Neukölln could only make guesses rather than throw light upon the case of Boxan, a worker, who was beaten up by three Communists. For the trial Boxan, who had been a Communist himself before he changed sides to the Nazis, revoked his testimony to the police so that the defendants had to be acquitted.

The national elections of 14 September 1930 also resulted in a fresh wave of political radicalism in Berlin. In the May 1928 elections the Communists, polling 615,000 votes, were still well behind the leading Social Democrats who also headed the city government. But in September 1930 they were just ahead of the SPD obtaining 739,000 votes against the latter's 738,000. However, the Nazi success was truly sensational. Their share of 15 per cent, it is true, did not match the 18.1 per cent achieved by them in the Reich as a whole. But their 395,000 votes is tenfold the number obtained in 1928. Their main rivals the German Nationalist People's Party (DNVP), which attracted 351,000 voters, was thus clearly left behind.

The Nazis gained the largest percentages in the well-to-do bourgeois suburbs of the city — like Steglitz, Charlottenburg, Wilmersdorf, Zehlendorf. But they also made considerable inroads in working-class districts. Here the Berlin Nazi Party (NSDAP), led by Joseph Goebbels since the end of 1926, from the start sought conflict with the Marxists and, judging from the number of street- and assembly-hall-battles, certainly succeeded in its objective. For years the traditional assembly place of the Nazi Party in the 'red wedding' district had been the *Kriegervereinshaus* in *Chausseestrasse*. As early as February 1927 the SA had risked a first fight with the Communists in their *Pharussäle* stronghold which later became glorified in Nazi literature. Now, in 1930, they gained 20,000 votes although it must be added that this was a mere fraction of the 99,000 Communist and 65,000 Social Democrat votes. The Communists hence retained their absolute dominance. A similar picture presented itself in the Friedrichshain district with its slums and seedy pubs near the *Schlesischer Bahnhof*. Here the swashbuckling young

15

SA-Sturmführer Horst Wessel roamed in 1928–9, winning young Communists over to the Brownshirts until in January 1930 he was murdered by a Communist rival. Eight months later the Nazi share in this district had risen to 24,000 as against 64,000 for the Communist Party (KPD) and 58,000 for the Social Democratic Party (SPD). The Nazis also obtained very good results in Spandau, an industrial and garrison district in the north-east of Berlin. Spandau was the birthplace of the first SA detachment in 1926. Four years later the Nazi share was 12,000 votes as against 26,000 for the SPD and 16,000 for the Communists.

The first reaction of the high-brow bourgeois–liberal press of Berlin to the Nazi success was one of stunned horror. The leader writer of the *Berliner Tageblatt* (16 September 1930) found it impossible to take in the 'monstrous fact' that 'six million and four hundred thousand voters in this highly civilised country had given their vote to the commonest, hollowest and crudest charlatanism'. On 21 September, Theodor Wolff, the paper's editor, added sarcastically and in a mood of artificial optimism: 'For the time being we allow ourselves to cling to the hope that later historians will see National Socialism not as a new phase, but as a new empty slogan of history'.

It took some time for insights, combined with self-criticism, to grow. Thus Hans Meisel wrote in *Vossische Zeitung* of 2 October 1930: 'Nothing has been more depressing to watch than the self-demolition of the bourgeoisie, the psychic suicide of an entire class. . . . The belief in the bourgeoisie's right to exist disintegrates even more rapidly than that in the bourgeois existence itself. . . . Large parts of middle-class youth no longer think in bourgeois terms. They think either Marxist or fascist.' The sociologist Professor Hans von Eckart, writing in the same paper on 20 November, tried to provide a more profound analysis of the September events:

We have entered a period of rapid movement. . . . Only those of our political parties have remained relatively stable which, like Social Democracy and [Catholic] Centre Party, keep their followers together *organisationally*, i.e. keep them occupied. Neither of these two parties has a really shining attraction anymore in terms of its ideas; they are incapable of issuing exciting slogans or of making promises about a splendid future. But they facilitate constant political *activity*; they organise and fill out the daily lives of their adherents. Party politics in these circles has a totally different meaning compared with notions held by the middle classes. Hundreds of thousands of functionaries are full of energy; they put before the followers a vivid illusion that they can be effective outside the process of work and of earning a living. Communists and National Socialists try to build up what Social Democracy has already achieved: a living movement which is confronted with new tasks every day. The people who are being wooed for these tasks are not told clearly what is to be; they are being given politically what they are denied by the State: organised intellectual leisure activities whatever they may be. This is not grand politics which shapes the state and the social order. . . . However, the desire of the masses to be *busy*, to participate, to be raptured, can no longer be overlooked. It is not a question of the leaders being successful, as they like to claim, but of the masses pushing into every direction where they are given opportunities for action and, at the same time, put under the spell of an idea. We have had plenty of discussion about the meaning of this idea, but we have paid very little attention to how it is to work itself out. Today the bourgeoisie watches helplessly the demise of the Democratic Party whose ideas were supposed to be so good. But the party's organisation was all the poorer, or to be blunt: totally inadequate; it failed to integrate its members and to provide them with political activity.

The Communists, von Eckart continued, knew how to occupy their adherents through constant activism.

And as, psychologically speaking, the Nazis are in a similar position, it is barely surprising that this party is successful. In terms of their social composition, [its members] are, above all, people who are either unemployed or non-unionised; in other words, they are people who have simply seized a first opportunity of participating and who have hitherto not yet been able to be politically active.

Von Eckart ended his article with gloomy predictions of a 'cultural crisis' resulting not only from mass unemployment, but also from the devaluation of labour more generally which pushed people towards the search for fulfillment in a political movement.

1.2. *Goebbels's Struggle for Berlin: Methods, Crises, Contradictions*

On 1 November 1930 Goebbels's bi-weekly *Der Angriff* appeared as a daily and in a larger format for the first time. This provided him as the editor with an opportunity to look back upon the modest beginnings of the Berlin NSDAP and SA which the Nazi movement had only recently left behind it. 'We barely succeeded in making ends meet', he wrote. 'But we opened our mouths all the more widely and shouted all the more loudly. The fewer there were of us, the more we gave the appearance of being many. We shouted and screamed; we fought elegantly or with heavy sabres, we used large calibres and poisoned arrows and, in this way, slowly made our way up.'

Like almost all other statements by the *Gauleiter* of Berlin, this one was also a half-truth. The mixture of cynicism and cockiness which since 1926–7 had marked the political agitation of this tiny, tremendously vain, aggressive and intellectually fertile young man who was an extraordinarily skilful orator and journalist had failed to produce electoral results in Berlin during the first two years. In the national elections of May 1928 the Nazis gained a mere 2.6 per cent of the total vote. Some eight months later, in December 1928, the share had risen to 5.7 per cent. Only when the disappointment and despair among the petty bourgeoisie and the unorganised blue-collar workers over their material plight assumed major proportions and when Hitler's party began to gain respectability through its struggle, in conjunction with Hugenberg's Nationalist Party (DNVP) and the *Stahlhelm* ex-Servicemen's Association, against the Young Plan reparations agreement, did the tide also turn in Berlin.

Now there was a better response to the provocative language and the demonstrations of Nazi power; to the methods of work at the grass-roots which had been copied from the Communists: regular meetings, rallies, demonstrations, outings, to the formation of political cells in apartment blocks and in the factories and the identification of regular meeting places ('SA pubs', 'SA-*Stammkneipen*'). This was also the soil in which Goebbels's propaganda ideas began to flourish. From February 1930, with the composition of the Horst Wessel Song, the cult of Nazi martyrs began to take root. There were the alleged scandals which *Der Angriff* kept on uncovering. Police and courts were constantly ridiculed. The paper published anti-Semitic cartoons of people in authority like the Jewish deputy police president Dr Bernhard Weiss. It did not matter to Goebbels that Weiss was a sincere democrat and a crime expert of international standing who, because of his incorruptible objectivity, also enjoyed a high reputation among his colleagues in Berlin. A Jew who occupied a key position in the Berlin police headquarters of 'Red' Prussia was an ideal target for Nazi clichés. 'Isidor' Weiss, as the Goebbels propaganda invariably called him, became the object of a vicious political pornography which also sought and found laughing support among the Communist and nationalist opponents of the Berlin police presidium.

In the semi-criminal milieu of some of the slum areas of Berlin, Goebbels could also count on gaining popularity by calling himself 'chief bandit' in the language of the local gangsters and by publicly bragging about the dozens of prosecutions which had been started against him. One of the most widely publicised cases was that brought against him by Reich President Paul von Hindenburg. It arose in connection with a cartoon in *Der Angriff* dealing with the government's acceptance of the Young Plan. The cartoon showed Hindenburg as a pitiless Germanic god who watches in cold blood how generations of Germans in chains are being led into slavery. The caption said: 'And the saviour is [passively] looking on.' At subsequent mass rallies, Goebbels — cocky, arrogant and provocative as ever — exploited the topic further: 'Who has enslaved the German people?', he asked. 'Was it me or he? Who should be put in the dock? Me or he?'

Later, on 1 June 1930, he noted in his diary:[2] 'Wonderful propaganda for us', following the end of the trial before the Moabit court with many correspondents in the press gallery. Although the state prosecutor had demanded a nine-months' prison sentence, Goebbels was fined a mere 800 marks. Five days later, *Der Angriff* rejoiced: 'A moral acquittal'; 'Simply devastating for Hindenburg's advisers', 'A massive advertisement for National Socialism in Berlin, more effective than fifty mass rallies'. The press carried photos of Goebbels triumphantly leaving the court building. He drove off in a Mercedes car

2. These and subsequent quotations are taken from diary fragments in Goebbels's hand, held by the Munich *Institut für Zeitgeschichte* and to be published shortly.

surrounded by jubilant supporters who had their arms raised for the 'Heil Hitler' salute.

In this way he succeeded time and again, at least outwardly, in making the police and the judiciary the laughing-stock of the public. However, it would be wrong to assume that the counter-measures of the Prussian authorities and state prosecutor remained ineffectual. Goebbels's diary again bears clear testimony to this. On 17 August 1930 he wrote: 'The trials worry me a lot. I feel like vomiting.' On 26 August he groaned when, in the middle of the election campaign, he had to appear before the courts and in two instances was fined 1,600 marks for making defamatory statements: 'The courts persecute me with prosecutions and hearings.' In short, this mockery of the police and the judiciary which allegedly provided free propaganda for the Nazis, was not genuine. Nor was it helpful to the party when, in the so-called 'Rötgenthal Trial', nine young SA men who had shot two members of the republican *Reichsbanner* paramilitary association, were given long hard labour sentences. The same applied to the trial of Ali Höhler, Horst Wessel's murderer, who revealed that one of the great 'martyrs' of the Berlin SA had had connections with prostitutes. Problems finally also arose for Goebbels when the NSDAP was shaken by serious intra-party crises which originated in Berlin in the summer of 1930.

During the election campaign the SA which in Berlin as elsewhere formed the activist hardcore of the Nazi movement underwent a process of ferment. A dare-devil actionism had been mobilised in the SA contingents which was based not so much on ideological conviction than on the experience of *bündische* comradeship and adventurism to be found among young nationalists of proletarian or bourgeois background. The *bündische* soldierly demeanour of the Free Corps movement was in fact more typical of many SA leaders (most of whom were former front-line officers of the First World War) than party loyalty.

The ex-captain Walter Stennes was the embodiment of this type of person. He had an incredible career behind him, before he assumed the position of Supreme Leader of the SA in Berlin and eastern Germany in 1928. As a front-line soldier of the First World War he was highly decorated and received several injuries. In 1919, undeterred and a skilled organiser, Stennes first formed a Free Corps together with his former subordinates. He defended the Republic against Spartacist insurgents in the Ruhr area. But after the Kapp Putsch of March 1920 he drifted towards the extreme Right. In 1923 he became entangled in a Putsch at Küstrin by illegal (Black) *Reichswehr* units. In this connection he had made Hitler's acquaintance. Later he put himself at the latter's disposal when the SA was being rebuilt after Hitler's release from Landsberg prison. Stennes saw himself as a revolutionary nationalist in a broad sense, but lacked a clear ideological commitment. This is also why he reacted all the more self-confidently and allergically to the manifestations of party corruption and a byzantine admiration of Hitler which was spreading in the NSDAP and in the Munich party headquarters in particular. One bone of contention among several was that Hitler had bought the Barlow Palais in the early summer of 1930. He began to turn it into an expensive and luxurious command centre for the NSDAP, known as the 'Brown House', while the Berlin SA was asked to make continual sacrifices. Stennes also felt aggrieved that the SA had not been taken into consideration for the selection of Nazi Reichstag candidates. Election to the Reichstag carried with it financial and legal privileges. At the end of August these tensions came out into the open. The Berlin SA refused to give protection to Nazi rallies, a task which had vastly increased during the run-up to the elections. Stennes called the SA contingents of the *Gau* Berlin, numbering some 2,000 men, together and put them under his exclusive leadership.

The SA leaders subsequently felt they were being kept under surveillance by the SS men who acted as guards at the *Gau* offices in *Hedemannstrasse*. Stennes ordered an SA contingent to occupy the offices during the night of 30/1 August 1930. There were bloody scuffles and the SA men, enraged by the Nazi functionaries, began to demolish the furniture. Goebbels was away on an election tour and the party secretary who was standing in for him felt obliged to call for police protection against the SA.

Goebbels and Hitler hurried to Berlin. Hitler sensed the rebellious mood of the SA. At first he tried to get rid of Stennes by offering him a ministerial post in the Brunswick state government. But Stennes was not prepared to abandon the SA leadership for Berlin, whereupon Hitler took the steam out of the revolt by granting the SA a number of its demands. Reconciliation was achieved in public with a handshake between Hitler and Stennes in the evening of 1 September. But the conflict continued to smoulder below the surface until there was a further eruption seven months later in the so-called 'Stennes Revolt'.

The SA had been moved by the question of whether the aims of the Hitler movement were guided by the idea of seizing power in parliament via the ballot box or through revolutionary action. Related to it was the problem of what importance was to be given to the notion of socialism within the NSDAP. Elections in 1928 and 1929 had shown, however, that votes were to be gained not among the urban industrial working class, but among the peasantry and the provincial middle classes. While the party's overall electoral strategy changed to take account of these realities, Berlin, with its peculiar social structure, remained the centre of Nazi agitation among the working class. The tone of this propaganda was revolutionary and socialist. In this respect Goebbels hardly differed from the Strasser brothers, Otto and Gregor, who through their Kampf-Verlag publishing house had for years been publishing papers like *Der Nationale Sozialist* as the organs of the Nazi Left. However, there was a marked rivalry between Goebbels's paper and the Strasser press. Also, sharp conflicts arose over whether the aims proclaimed in the Party programme took precedence over loyalty to Hitler as the *Führer*. There ensued a major dispute between Hitler and Otto Strasser who, as *spiritus rector* and editor of his Kampf-Verlag papers, openly challenged Hitler's political opportunism with the slogan 'ministerial seats or revolution?' At the end of June 1930 Hitler wrote to Goebbels ordering him to oust the 'salon Bolshevik' and 'intellectual' ('*Literat*') Strasser from the party. Goebbels had been an arch enemy of Strasser's and was delighted to oblige. Strasser now tried to found his own party, called 'Revolutionary National Socialists'. On 4 July 1930 he published an appeal 'National Socialists are leaving the NSDAP'. But he failed like Stennes, with whom he collaborated for a while. As early as 1930 the integrating power of Hitler who was moreover able to allocate posts and parliamentary seats proved stronger in the Nazi Party than the power of ideology.

Nevertheless, the tension continued between the facade of legality and conservatism, on the one hand, and pseudo-socialist and revolutionary aspirations, on the other. This tension became particularly acute in Berlin where Goebbels's combative tactics and the activities of the newly founded National Socialist Factory Cell Organization (NSBO) encountered the leaders of the Nazi caucus in the Reichstag which since September 1930 had grown to 107 MPs. These leaders were more cautious and concerned about their reputation. Their tactics were geared towards possible government participation and towards preparing the ground for political talks which Hitler and Göring now began to have increasingly with representatives of the government, the army and industry.

One of the milestones in this development, extensively commented upon in the Berlin press with a considerable divergence of views, was the legality oath which Hitler swore on 25 September before the Reich Court at Leipzig. On this occasion he appeared in a trial against three officers who had joined the Nazi Party and declared: 'Here I stand swearing an oath before God, the Almighty. I say to you that, once I shall have come to power by legal means, I shall by legal authority institute state courts which will try under the law those who are responsible for the misfortune of our people.' This appeared to be, at least outwardly, a clear statement that power was to be achieved by legal means and that the putschist tradition of 1923 had been left behind. But then followed a sentence which was evidently designed to appease the revolutionaries in the party: 'It is possible that, [quite] legally, a few heads will roll in the sand on that occasion.'[3] Hitler's 'legality oath' received much applause in the army and in circles of the conservative 'National Opposition'. The republicans on the other hand rightly remained suspicious. Goebbels took Hitler's last sentence as his guideline, adding cynically: 'Now we are strictly legal, to hell with legality [*egal legal*].'[4] In fact, however, he was disquieted by Hitler's legality tactics. His suspicions were aroused even more by the busy opportunism of Hermann Göring who posed as Hitler's

3. See, e.g., *Illustrierte Republikanische Zeitung*, 14.6.1930.
4. See P. Bucher, *Der Reichswehrprozess*, Boppard 1967, pp. 237ff.

regent in Berlin and untiringly tried to establish contacts with the conservative elites and with industry. At the beginning of December 1930 Gottfried Feder, the party's expert on economic theory, declared in the Reichstag that the NSDAP rejected all socialist tendencies. On 4 December Goebbels noted in his diary: 'Terrible. I am beyond myself with rage against him'.

Meanwhile the policy of the Berlin NSDAP clearly deviated from the Headquarter's line. When in the middle of October the Berlin metal-workers staged a strike, the Nazi factory cells fully identified themselves with the strike and even tried to outdo the radicalism of Communist propaganda. The Berlin *Gau* leadership issued a warning that 'strike-breakers will be excluded from the party'. *Der Angriff* added: 'The stock-market hyenas are sitting in London and New York's Wall Street for whose benefit the German worker is expected to accept a cut in his already meagre living standard.' Commenting on 18 October 1930, the conservative *Berliner Tageszeitung* thought the NSDAP's wholesale adoption of the strike propaganda of the Free Trade Unions and the Communists was a renewed piece of evidence 'that the purely socialist tendencies within the National Socialist Party are very much stronger than is still taken to be the case by many people'. Two days earlier the liberal *Vossische Zeitung* had raised the question of whether *Der Angriff*'s rude language was compatible with the interviews which Hitler had recently given to correspondents of the Anglo-Saxon Rothermere- and Hearst-presses and in which he tried to 'prove to just those "stock-market hyenas" that National Socialism today presented the only dam against social rebellion and a Bolshevisation of Germany'. In the middle of October Hitler gave an interview to the London *Times* in which he even tried to tone down and minimise his anti-Semitism. He assured the correspondent that he did not wish to be associated with pogroms. His maxim was 'Germany to the Germans' and his attitude towards the Jews was merely guided by the question of whether the Jews adhered to this principle. National Socialists had no objections to 'decent Jews'. However, should they link up with Bolshevism, as many — he asserted — unfortunately tended to do, they would have to be regarded as enemies.[5]

5. See R. Scheringer, *Das große Los*, Hamburg 1959, p. 236. Scheringer was one of the defendants in the Reichswehr trial.

Some national–conservative papers, which found the noisy
anti-Semitism of the Nazis repulsive, badly misinterpreted such
news. Thus we read in Arthur Mahraun's *Der Jungdeutsche* on 18
October 1930: 'Adolf Hitler has abandoned anti-Semitism; this
much one can now say with certainty. But officially [he has done
so] for the moment only *vis-à-vis* foreign representatives and
above all for the consumption of the jobbers in the City and in
Wall Street. At home however National Socialist supporters
continue to be taken for a ride with anti-Semitic slogans.'

In this period of economic crisis and mass unemployment, the
economic programme of the NSDAP inevitably attracted the
greatest interest. On 10 November four well-known professors
of economics — Heinrich Herkner (Berlin), Christian Eckert
(Cologne), Alfred Weber (Heidelberg) and Götz Briefs (Berlin)
— wrote an open letter to the Nazi Reichstag faction. In it they
asked for clarification as to whether the NSDAP still adhered to
the hypothesis that 'interest slavery' should be 'broken' and that
interest rates be limited to four per cent. Then they explained
what, in economic terms, this would mean to small businesses
and to the house-owning *Mittelstand*.

The sensational success of the NSDAP in the September
elections, which even surprised the party, turned the Hitler
movement into a potential partner in a coalition government. It
raised more and more insistently the question of whether the
Nazis were capable of sharing government responsibility and
which were their objectives. However, those who put these
questions still misjudged the character of the National Socialist
lust for power which both Hitler and Goebbels equally represented. Whatever the terms and the timing of a Nazi participation in the government, the basic aim was the further erosion of
the Republic's stability — especially in Prussia and especially in
Berlin.

1.3. *The Prussian Government and Police as the Main Opponents*

At the end of March 1930, the last Reich Cabinet that had been
formed on a parliamentary basis and had been led by a Social
Democratic Chancellor, Hermann Müller, collapsed. It was replaced by the government of Chancellor Heinrich Brüning

which had been nominated by President Hindenburg and in whose formation the *Reichswehr* leadership had played a prominent part. There was no Social Democrat in the new Cabinet. Instead it relied on representatives of the bourgeois centre and the moderate Right. It did not have a solid parliamentary base, but depended on a changing majority of parties which were prepared to tolerate it. If this became impossible, it would govern without parliament by means of emergency decrees signed by the President and based on Article 48 of the Weimar Constitution. Consequently the Brüning Cabinet was largely dependent on Hindenburg and his advisers. When on 18 July Brüning decided to dissolve the Reichstag and fresh elections were called for September, this development was a result of the new constitutional structure. Meanwhile Prussia, which comprised almost two thirds of the Reich in terms of size and population, was led by a stable parliamentary government under a Social Democratic Minister President, Otto Braun. It relied on the support of unambiguously republican parties: the SPD, the Catholic Centre and the German Democratic Party (DDP). Most of the Reich and Prussian ministries were situated in Berlin side-by-side in the *Wilhelmstrasse*, and it was in the capital that the contrast between a Reich Cabinet under Brüning which gravitated towards the Right and a left-wing Prussian government became particularly marked from the summer of 1930 onwards. Divergent attitudes towards the Nazi threat, which had greatly increased in the September elections, constituted an important point of friction.

The bourgeois–conservative parties which supported the Brüning Cabinet were in principle prepared to bring the Nazis into the government. They hoped that giving them political responsibility would neutralise their demagogy. The Social Democrats in the Prussian government, on the other hand, felt a deep distrust of the Nazis. They were also determined to make no concessions where the constitutional order was being violated or where the esteem for the Republic was being undermined. To be sure, everybody realised that, if elections for the Prussian Diet had been held in September 1930, there would have been a seismic shift in the political balance similar to that in the Reichstag and this would have pulled the rug from under Braun's feet. This realisation was enough to weaken the political legitimation of the Prussian government. But Braun could also argue that up to the end of the current legislative period of the Diet in the spring of 1932 it was all the more important to master the economic crisis and to resist the political radicalisation which it promoted.

This was essentially also Braun's position who was probably the most powerful political figure of Social Democracy during the Weimar period. He was called the 'Red Tsar of Prussia' because of his authoritarian style of government. Even his conservative opponents did not deny him their respect. Braun had always considered it important that the Prussian Ministry of the Interior was in the hands of a reliable Social Democrat.

Following the Kapp Putsch in 1920 the post had been filled by Carl Severing for the next six years. From the autumn of 1926 to February 1930 Albert Grzesinski had been Prussian Minister of the Interior. Both men were resolute Social Democrats who promoted with much circumspection the reform of the bureaucracy and above all the police. Severing was more politically-minded in tackling these reforms and more prepared and able to conclude compromises. Grzesinski was tougher and combined, like Braun, a loyal adherence to Social Democratic principles with a marked Prussian-authoritarian notion of the state. In order to strengthen the republican leadership of his ministry, Grzesinski had elevated a reliable democrat, Dr Wilhelm Abegg, to the position of State Secretary and head of the Police Department. Abegg provided a continuity of republicanism even when Grzesinski had a weak successor in Prof. Heinrich Waentig. In 1925–6 Grzesinski had been police president of Berlin for eighteen months. He therefore knew the Prussian police particularly well and appreciated its significance for the protection of the Republic. The Berlin police presidium at *Alexanderplatz* was the nerve-centre of the Prussian police and represented by far the largest police authority in Germany. There were some 21,000 officials, employees and labourers, among them 14,000 uniformed officers of the *Schutzpolizei* (with 3,000 commanders). One third of these lived in garrisons on special alert (*Bereitschaftspolizei*). There were also some 3,000 CID officers and some 300 were working in the political department (IA). The Social Democrat Zörgiebel had been heading the presidium for many years. However, there was a feeling that he had become worn down and that he tended to take controlling the

27

Communists and the successor organisation of the *Rotfrontkämp-ferbund* (the CP's paramilitary arm) which had been banned in 1929 more seriously than combatting the right-wing radical Nazis. Nevertheless, in Berlin, Zörgiebel was the main target for the SA and the NSDAP. He had been instrumental in banning the Berlin NSDAP in 1927–8 after major disturbances. In June 1930, following the Bavarian example, the SA had also been prohibited to wear uniforms.

If Goebbels, after the electoral triumph of the NSDAP in September 1930, therefore demanded the replacement of the Prussian government, his demand was motivated by very concrete experiences with the Berlin police. As he put it in *Der Angriff* on 5 October: 'Prussia is the key to gaining power in Germany. Whoever possesses Prussia, possesses the Reich. And the path to power in Prussia is via the conquest of Berlin. A Reich Cabinet which disagrees with the Prussian government will be the prisoner of the Berlin police president.' A month later fire-red posters appeared, inviting to a Nazi rally on 5 November in the Berlin *Sportpalast* and carrying the slogan: 'Masses come out. The struggle for Prussia is beginning!' Goebbels was to be the main speaker. Other speakers were Wilhelm Kube, the *Gauleiter* of the *Kurmark* and Edmund Heines who had been convicted of political murder and had been released on probation in 1929, only to gain a seat in the Reichstag in September 1930. Heines announced in his speech that the 'Red Prussian government' would be swept aside.

Braun was not particularly impressed by this campaign. When, on 15 October, the Nazi faction in the Reichstag demanded that the ban on SA uniforms be lifted, he remained unmoved: 'What has led to this ban, is above all the intolerable terror which you [National Socialists] . . . have exerted against those holding other political views. At the moment there is an even stronger justification for maintaining this ban.' Braun also reaffirmed on this occasion the ban on Prussian civil servants to belong to the Communist or Nazi parties and demonstrated how little he believed in Hitler's 'legality oath'. 'The situation', he said, 'is now so serious, that it amounts to a crime against the German people if the crisis is exploited for the purposes of unrestrained demagogy.' When the Nazis finally put another motion that the Prussian Diet be dissolved and asserted noisily that Braun should not remain 'glued to his seat', the Minister-President replied: 'You can really dispense with these cheap jokes. Without wishing to sound arrogant, I am of the opinion that my having stuck to my post for so long has been for the best of the German people. If we had had a similar series of government crises in the largest state of the Reich as occurred at Reich level, the German economy would probably be in a worse state.'[6]

Braun's view of the situation was also informed by events which had happened in Berlin two days earlier during the opening of the new Parliament. The 107-man Nazi faction wanted to make a spectacular entry in the presence of the correspondents of the national and international press in the gallery. The Nazis had been instructed to appear in their brown shirts, but to hide them under their jackets. At the start of the session no brown shirt was to be seen in the debating chamber. But as the correspondent of the *Vossische Zeitung* reported, the entry of the Nazis was 'rather more comic'. Their behaviour seemed 'a bit odd and also a bit ridiculous'.

A parallel action in the streets of Berlin was more successful, even if it had not been staged by the *Gau* leadership but had rather resulted from an initiative by radical SA groups and Nazi students.While the police were busy putting up barriers around the Reichstag and to keep onlookers, who wished to see the arrival of the deputies, at bay, groups of youths went on the rampage in the shopping area at *Potsdamer Platz* and in *Leipziger Strasse*. Within a short time, they had pulled up cobblestones to smash the windows of the Wertheim department store and a whole string of other Jewish shops. The police were too late to prevent this outrage. Over a hundred mainly young participants were arrested, and it was found that about half of these were card-carrying members of the NSDAP.

As Grzesinski wrote to Braun that same evening: 'It is necessary to be tough, as tough as iron, in such difficult times.' The leader of the police forces in charge of security in the government quarters should be sent on indefinite leave 'tomorrow' and 'Comrade Zörgiebel' should also be asked to go. 'The issue is more important than persons.' For some time the police had failed to show the mailed fist to the Nazis. Grzesinski was

6. Thus the report in *Vossische Zeitung*, 16.10.1930.

particularly disquieted by declarations of pro-Nazi sympathies on the part of individual police officers who should be disciplined most severely. 'To remain carefree', he concluded, 'is a crime against the state today.'[7]

Ten days later Braun announced changes in the Prussian top executive. Severing was recalled to become Minister of the Interior. Grzesinski was nominated Berlin police president. The republican press approved of this swift move. As the *Frankfurter Zeitung* put it: 'Herr Braun knows how to govern in Prussia.'[8] Goebbels had also immediately grasped the implications of the change. On 27 October he noted in his diary: 'Severing Prussian Minister of the Interior; Grzesinski Berlin police president. That's going to be a lovely winter. Nominations exclusively directed against us.'

Throughout October and November, the police were given plenty of opportunity to make good the mistakes of 13 October. Thus for 18 October Thomas Mann, the novelist, was billed to give a lecture in a hall at *Unter den Linden* in the centre of Berlin. He talked about the spiritual and political situation of the age. He used the occasion to pay his respects to the Social Democrats and their support of intellectual freedom. The demagogic activism of the Nazis, on the other hand, was dubbed by him as 'orgiastic'. There were catcalls and then disturbances by Nazi students and intellectuals. This time the police acted without delay. Order was restored and Thomas Mann was able to finish his speech.

On 12 November, then, at the start of the winter semester, members of the Socialist Students' League distributed leaflets in which they warned against the dangerous growth of Nazism at the Humboldt University. Groups of Nazi students tried to prevent the distribution and physically attacked the socialist students. The ensuing brawl escalated and spread to the gardens in front of the building and to the building itself. The University's president, Professor Deissmann, who vainly tried to mediate between the two sides, was also being threatened. The commander of the Berlin police, Heimannsburg, personally

7. Bundesarchiv Koblenz, Kleine Erwerbungen no. 144, unpubl. notes by Grzesinski of 1933 in which this letter is quoted.

8. Quoted in H. Schulze, *Otto Braun oder Preussens demokratische Sendung*, Frankfurt 1977, p. 643.

30

directed the police intervention which restored law and order in the University. However, he could not prevent the sharp differences of opinion within the student body from erupting again on the following day: groups of students confronting each other menacingly and shouting either 'Jews out' or 'Nazis out'.

Goebbels hoped that *Der Angriff*, to be published as a daily from 1 November, would give a fresh boost to Nazi propaganda. He exhorted the editors that it was now all the more important to increase the paper's circulation by provocative bluntness and sensationalism. On 5 November the paper began a new series of articles against 'Isidor'. As Weiss, the vice-president of the Berlin police, was beyond reproach, alleged misdemeanours of his brother were dredged up. As Goebbels recorded in his diary on 6 November: '*Angriff* marvellous. Isidor will be obliterated.' However, the new head of the Berlin police presidium was not a man to hold back, and he showed cunning. On 10 November he imposed a seven-day ban on *Der Angriff*. He based his decision not on the recent campaign against his deputy. This would merely have been grist to Goebbels's mill. Rather he referred to a small back-page item relating to an earlier incident: his predecessor Zörgiebel had been a witness at a trial in the course of which he had been slapped in the face by a Communist. On 8 November *Der Angriff* commented on this incident: 'Seldom, and yet from time to time, the actions of Communists are not wholly unsympathetic to us.' Grzesinski argued that 'these words express direct approval of an act of violence committed by a Communist against the former police president because of the latter's political activity which is punishable in accordance with Paragraph 5, Section 4 of the Law for the Protection of the Republic.'[9]

Goebbels was thunder-struck and recorded in his diary: 'Disastrous news: *Angriff* banned for one week. Just because of a ridiculous remark about the slap in Zörgiebel's face. Great depression; losses of 15,000 marks. And all this now!' A further setback came on 13 November which Goebbels recorded as follows: 'Rally in the 'New World' [assembly hall] banned. That is Grzesinski's [work], that arch proletarian.' The Nazi *Gauleiter* of Berlin planned his revenge.

9. Quoted in *Der Angriff*, 11.11.1930.

1.4. *The Boycott of Remarque's Film* All Quiet on the Western Front

On 4 December 1930 the première of the German version of Erich Maria Remarque's American-produced film *All Quiet on the Western Front* took place at the *Mozartsaal* cinema on *Nollendorf-platz*. This version had been produced by *Ufa* and the Board of Film Censors in the Reich Ministry of the Interior, which had to certify the film, had had no objections. *Ufa* had cut or corrected some footage from the American original which might have been interpreted as anti-German. The premiere passed without incident. The audience was deeply moved. On 6 November Heinz Pol wrote in the *Vossische Zeitung* that, although the film followed the novel only in general terms and often presented a rather crude version of its contents, it nevertheless reflected the spirit of the novel particularly in its most disturbing sequences:

> The metamorphosis of enthusiastic sixth-formers into front soldiers who do their duty because they are forced to; the transformation of an idealistic youth to a steel-helmeted man in field-grey uniform who has seen the most horrific thing a man will ever see . . . The frightful irrationality of war emerges most clearly in the film's big battle scenes which belong to the technically most grandiose and most moving which we have experienced in sound-film so far.

Certainly the sober unheroic portrayal of trench warfare on the Western front was a realistic corrective to the militaristic literature of Ernst Jünger, Franz Schauwecker and others whose glorifications of war were promoted on a massive scale.

Goebbels had long been a film enthusiast. He loved to relax in the evening after the tiring daily routine as a politician and propagandist by going to the cinema. He was captivated by *Fridericus Rex*, starring Otto Gebühr, and *Liebling der Götter* with Emil Jannings. But he was particularly attracted by the heroic and the sophisticatedly sentimental. Nor was he a narrow-minded stickler when it came to film and theatre. He did not refrain from criticising even those productions by his own brain-child, the Nazi theatre in Berlin, which, though ideologically proper, were found lacking on artistic grounds. When this theatre put on a production by a young and overambitious Nazi director which gave a radical reinterpretation of Friedrich Schiller's *Die Räuber*, including a portrayal of Spiegelberg as the 'Eternal Jew', *Der Angriff* praised this sordid piece exuberantly; but Goebbels internally reprimanded this 'anti-Semitism of the rascals' and its lack of professionalism, as he recorded in his diary on 17 October and 3 November 1930.

Goebbels was no doubt receptive to the fascinating American style of *All Quiet on the Western Front*. However, the film itself was merely a pretext when he decided to launch a spectacular protest against it. His diary indicates that he did not see the première of the film on 4 December. His information about it was based on hearsay, possibly on newspaper reports in the national press which in previous weeks had made critical remarks about the American original.

Since 3 December the Nazi parliamentary faction had reassembled in Berlin in which Goebbels, much to his chagrin, had not been able to gain much influence so far. Here was therefore an opportunity to show off in front of the party bosses from all over Germany. Even more tempting was the new platform of this protest which was difficult to control by the police and which had not been tested before: a cinema plunged into darkness. Friday, 5 December was to be the evening. Goebbels, a few Nazi MPs and several dozens of SA men and party members in civilian clothes, in all some 200 of them, had gone to the *Mozartsaal* and bought seats in different parts of the cinema, especially on the balcony. The film had been screened for no more than ten minutes when the racket began. Loud shouts like 'filthy film', 'pigsty', 'throw the Jews out' could be heard blending with the noise of exploding grenades on the sound-track. Smoke-bombs were thrown from the balcony. Paper bags with sneezing powder were tossed into the audience. White mice were let loose by Goebbels's men in the stalls. There was pandemonium and the film had to be stopped. Münchmeyer, a parson and Nazi MP made a protest speech from the balcony. Goebbels shouted: 'Hitler is in the front of the gates of Berlin.' Viewers who protested against the racket were beaten up. The patron had no choice but to call the police and to have the cinema cleared out with truncheons. Goebbels later sarcastically commented in his diary. 'The cinema has been turned into a madhouse a mere ten minutes after the start of the

33

film. . . . The Jews try to make themselves invisible [*klein und hässlich*]. Thousands of people enjoy the spectacle in a mood of satisfaction . . . Afterwards I sit in a café with my lads; experiences are swapped; it is hilariously funny, but everything has worked well . . . Our action in the *Mozartsaal* is the topic of the day. The press is teeming with rage or full of enthusiasm. Once again I have had the right scent. Our MPs are exuberant. This was a [good] piece.'

Der Angriff wrote sanctimoniously under the heading 'Storm of Protest in the *Mozartsaal*: 'When the cowardice of the volunteers was shown on the screen, the audience raised a storm of protest which forced the cinema owner to interrupt the screening. Serious brawls developed which were provoked by Jews and in which the police had to intervene. . . . There is such a blatant tendency in this film to denigrate the German spirit [*deutsches Wesen*] that one must not be surprised, if the *Volk* takes matters into its own hands.'

The people of Berlin wondered if the film would be screened on the following night. The conservative press, too, demanded that Grzensinski should ban the film. The latter had no inclination to give in to the pressure which Goebbels had set in train. He persuaded the patron to carry on and promised police protection. There were renewed riots in the evenings of Saturday, Sunday and Monday especially by opponents of the film. Goebbels, surrounded by his cohorts, posed as a people's tribune. The Berlin correspondent of *The Times* sent the following report to London on 8 December:

Agitation of the self-styled 'nationally-minded' section of the Berlin population against the film *All Quiet on the Western Front* was continued today. A demonstration against this evening's performance of the film at the Mozart-Saal in the Nollendorf Platz was openly organised by Herr Goebbels, the Berlin Nazi leader, with the aid of his newspaper *Der Angriff*. The Nollendorf Platz is most unsuitable for mass demonstrations and a strong cordon of the police protected the theatre. In spite of a discouraging drizzle, youthful Nazis gathered outside the cordon, shouted 'Germany awake!', sang Nazi songs, and called the police 'Bloodhounds' and added their usual embroideries to the *Angriff's* views on 'dirty Jews'. When Herr Goebbels arrived in a motor-car, a mass of hundreds surged across the street and surrounded the car, arms upraised in the Fascist salute. In a couple of minutes, by a neat police manoeuvre, the motor-car, Herr Goebbels and the bulk of the crowd had all been pushed up a narrow half-street bounded by the embankment wall, from the Nollendorf Platz towards the Wittenberg Platz. There was no returning through the cordon. Thereafter the Nazis were allowed to demonstrate to their hearts' content in the Wittenberg Platz, where Herr Goebbels spoke, and to march round and round an area of about six blocks between the two squares. Section after section was formed, with 'storm detachment leaders' in the front ranks. Behind, in columns of fours, followed a collection of nationally-minded — mostly youths, with a sprinkling of middle-aged men and women, and an occasional dog.

Der Angriff then called for a further and even bigger demonstration to be held on 9 December in front of the *Mozartsaal*. As the *Vossische Zeitung* suspected on 10 November, the Nazis were intent on using violence in order to prove to people at home and abroad that law and order had broken down in the capital and that mob-rule had begun. Of the 60,000 demonstrators, which *Der Angriff* had talked about, only 6–8,000 turned up. Nevertheless, Grzesinski was not prepared to give Goebbels further room for manoeuvre. On 10 December demonstrations were banned from the whole of Berlin.

However, the Reich government was unwilling to go along with this proposal. As early as 9 December Alfred Hugenberg, the leader of the DNVP had sent a telegram to Reich President Hindenburg, asking him to end the film scandal through his personal intervention. At the same time the *Reichswehr* appeared on the scene. The Reich Ministry of the Interior also received submissions from the *Stahlhelm* ex-Servicemen's Association and the League of German Officers (DOB), together with urgent requests from a number of *Länder*, among them Thuringia and Brunswick, where Nazis occupied the post of Interior Minister. Put under pressure in this way and probably also gently egged on by Brüning, Reich Interior Minister Josef Wirth, a member of the Centre Party and until now a staunch supporter of the Republic, asked the Board of Film Censors to examine the film again. On 11 December the censors issued a ban on grounds that the film endangered 'the German image abroad'. On the following day, a week after the start of Goebbels's protests, *Der Angriff* announced in giant letters: 'Grzesinski defeated.' The

35

Vossische Zeitung wrote on the same day that the Board's verdict could 'not be accepted as an objective view. It is the product of political pressure.' The paper believed that the views of the *Reichswehr* Ministry had once more been decisive. There was also the desire of the Reich Cabinet 'not to burden the host of problems which threatened the cohesion of the government coalition with an ideological struggle which the film was beginning to unleash. It has decided to take the object of conflict off the screen in order to buy peace for the moment.' *The Times* of 12 December 1930 added the following comment: '[The ban] is generally interpreted as a capitulation of authority to the young men (of whom the great majority never knew the War and only a tiny minority can have seen the film) who have lately been parading round Berlin.'

The *Petit Parisien* wrote on the same day that 'fear of further Nazi demonstrations appears to have been the sole reason behind the [government's] capitulation'. Referring to foreign reactions the *Vossische Zeitung* finally concluded on 13 December: 'The ban has brought no benefit to German prestige abroad; nor has it enhanced the authority of the Reich government at home.'

National Socialism and the Weimar Republic

2.1. *The Historical Preconditions of National Socialism*

National Socialism emerged in Germany after the First World War during a period of worldwide economic recession and against the background of a general crisis of modernity and civilisation. These developments also undermined liberal traditions and democratic constitutions in other European countries and furthered the rise of authoritarian and fascist movements. International Communism which had arisen from the world war in the wake of the 1917 Revolution in Russia moreover presented a fresh challenge. Yet nowhere else was 'fascism' able to assert itself as massively as in Germany; nowhere else did it develop a more perfect system of wielding power; nowhere else was its magnetic force and its aggressive dynamism stronger. The factors, which cannot be separated from each other, force the analyst of the preconditions of National Socialism to combine the examination of the general European crisis, which was rooted in the pre-1914 period, but became clearly discernible during and after the First World War, with Germany's national history and its peculiar divergence from the West, especially during the interwar years. There are also methodological reasons which appear to make it advisable to choose a relatively narrow timescale for our analysis of the preconditions of Nazism. At least they modify older approaches in the tradition of American intellectual history which attempted to draw a line from Herder or Fichte to Hitler or from Nietzsche to Hitler.

The problematical nature of this latter perspective emerges if if one studies the modern populist ideological structure of National Socialism. Its *Weltanschauung* had barely anything in common with the 'old' school of culture and rigorous intellectual discourse which still informed the major political thought systems of the first half of the nineteenth century. Nazi ideology was almost totally a product of mass culture and political semi-illiteracy which proliferated since the late nineteenth century; it did not represent the epitome of contemporary knowledge and cognition, but unsophisticated sloganeering which drew on the 'scrapheap of ideas current in this period' (J. Fest). What made Nazi ideology compelling was not its penetrating intellectualism or the cohesion of its system of ideas. Rather it was the gripping effectiveness with which popularised snippets of ideas and dogmas of salvation of a certain kind were combined with a political–emotional attachment. What was decisive was not whether these ideas were suited to transmit insights or even comprehensive utopias based on rational argument, but could be used for the deliberate simplification of political world-views and for the creation of a political myth for the masses.

If one is trying to trace the historical roots of National Social-ism, particular reference has to be made to the type of modern political myth creation which Georges Sorel described in his 1908 *Reflections on Violence*. The so-called 'integral nationalism' of the Pan-Germans of the Wilhelmine days and, above all, that of Georg von Schoenerer in German-speaking Austria-Hungary comes into this category. In France it was the conservative-republican nationalism of Charles Maurras and his *Action Fran-çaise*, in Italy the pre-fascist concepts of the *Associatione Nationa-lista*. As Fritz Stern's analysis of the spokesmen of a conservative-*völkisch* cultural pessimism in pre-1914 Germany has shown, almost all essential elements of the late Nazi ideology were to be found in the radical positions of ideological protest movements, such as in the writings of Paul de Lagarde. These were: a virulent anti-Semitism, a blood-and-soil ideology, the notion of a master race, the idea of territorial, acquisition and settlement in the East. These ideas were embedded in a popular national-ism which was vigorously anti-modernist, anti-humanist and pseudo-religious.

Within the context of the general cultural crisis which had set in before 1914 Germany no doubt presented a special case, where by the turn of the century criticism of bourgeois security and rationality had become vehement and widespread. This criticism also expressed itself in various life reform movements and avant-garde artistic trends, in the pedagogical reform movement and, above all, in the Youth Movement which did not exist in a comparable shape outside Germany. Thus creativity was pitted against knowledge; experience against education, stiff uprightness against insight, dogmatism against pragmatism. They became the new lodestars among large sections of middle-class youth especially at high schools and universities long before the First World War gave a further boost to them, channelling much of the originally unpolitical rigorousness and neo-idealism into a nationalist radicalism. There were a number of reasons for the strength of this rejection of bourgeois culture which the First World War and its consequences were later to obliterate. One of these reasons was related to the educational substance of German idealism which had been uncritically and dogmatically instilled through schools and universities. More importantly, there was the culture of the epigones of the Bismarckian age and the superficial patriotic pathos of Wilhelmine bourgeois society which no doubt deserved a critical attitude. The official bourgeois public largely fed on empty phrase-making and tended to paper over the serious internal conflicts and tensions which bedevilled the political and social system of the Second Empire.

In the attempt at tracing the specifically German roots of National Socialism, much has been written about these inner fissures and 'dislocations' (Ralf Dahrendorf). The problem must be related above all to the dynamic of Germany's rise as an industrial and military power after 1870. It was in the context of this development that the political and social structures were, to some extent, deliberately petrified and certainly lagged far behind the rapid change in the economic sphere. Germany moved up economically and power-politically to approach the might of the first-rank global and industrial powers of the age; but at home considerable feudal privileges, the hegemonic political influence of the East Elbian *Junker* and the prerogatives of the Prusso-German military monarchy remained. The bourgeoisie remained exposed to aristocratic-military, authoritarian and statist structures and modes of consciousness which were transmitted from above and were legally and ideologically sanctioned. Meanwhile the growing mass of Social Democratic industrial workers was subjected for more than a decade to the anti-Socialist Laws whose impact could be felt long after the lapse in 1890 of this discriminatory legislation in such areas as electoral laws, police behaviour, judiciary practice and public consciousness in general.

These and other domestic divisions and contradictions of the Hohenzollern monarchy could be felt in 1914. If the outbreak of the First World War was greeted by many Germans as a kind of 'purifying thunderstorm', it was not only because they held high hopes of nationalist and imperialist consolidation, but also for socio-political or more vaguely 'spiritual' reasons. It was not only many intellectuals, but also various spokesmen of the working-class movement who, in the autumn of 1914, promised that this war would lead to the Germans finding themselves; would result in an intensification of patriotism and, above all, in a disappearance of class conflicts and status differences in the melting pot of the folk community. Both Hitler and a broad phalanx of conservative and 'national–revolutionary' movements later drew upon this instinctive 'war socialism' and upon the idea of a Sacred Peace (*Burgfrieden*) between the political parties which the Kaiser had proclaimed in August 1914. The German 'Ideas of 1914' were seen as the historic antidote to the French 'Ideas of 1789'.

Whatever the pre-1914 ideological precursors and structural preconditions of the Weimar period, only the First World War was to cause the decisive seismic shift in the country's political culture. This was the soil in which Nazism was to grow. The war experience of the Franco-Prussian War of 1870–1 had not been particularly intense and had faded from memory since then. It was this first total war of 1914–18 which produced an incomparably stronger and more comprehensive nationalist integration, through the war experience, of a society which had meanwhile become a mass society. Even the relatively immobile rural strata which had hitherto shown a low level of political consciousness, were seized by this feeling. Young peasants and land labourers returned with changed personalities, after the war had torn them from the slow-moving pace of provincial life and had thrown them into the 'wide world' and onto the stage of fateful national developments. Ex-servicemen's associations in the countryside thenceforth symbolised almost everywhere that a sphere which had adhered to largely unpolitical life-styles far removed from the centre of national affairs had become politicised primarily via the nationalist experience of the war. This had immediate consequences for the latent potential of fascism in the rural parts of Germany. Both the central government and the national political parties had traditionally neglected the provinces and this neglect created an even stronger sense of grievance after 1918 than had existed before the First World War. Both in Germany and Italy, but also in Rumania and Hungary a potential of rural protesters who had been shaped by the war experience provided massive recruitment grounds for the incipient fascist movements. They succeeded in rallying many of the young peasants and land labourers who had returned from the front and had become amenable to political mobilisation.

To be sure, what can be said about the roots of National Socialism and related movements in Germany and elsewhere in this particular case has a more general validity: the sociological prototype member of these movements was the demobbed front soldier who either could not, or did not want to, return to civilian life. Instead he continued a life of adventure in the free camps and paramilitary associations which transposed to peacetime politics the experience of comradeship in the trenches, of a division of the world into friends and foes and of modern methods of combat. That their style of political combat was derived from the wartime experience is evidenced by the type of civil war which they waged, the ruthless murder of alleged traitors (*Fememorde*) and the terroristic penal expeditions launched against political opponents. These modes of conduct were just as familiar to the Free Corps and paramilitary leagues in Germany as they were to the Italian *squadristi* or the Iron Guards in Rumania and reflect the similarity in the style of combat which had been inspired by the war experience. Italian Fascists and German National Socialists thereby exploited the weakness and tolerance of the liberal-democratic constitutional state in which they operated. Moreover they could count on the basic support of the conservative leadership in the army and the bureaucracy which voiced no more than a cautious criticism of the 'uncouth' methods of the fascists. The latter presented themselves to a frightened bourgeoisie as the real guarantors of law and order in the struggle against revolutionary socialists and Communists; they posed as fighting associations which would restore national and social unity and replace the allegedly corrupt party democracies whose weakness one derided.

Another typical feature was the copying of certain stylistic elements of behaviour developed by revolutionary socialism, anarchism or syndicalism. There was also the often prominent role of a charismatic leader and of a propaganda and rhetoric which assumed pseudo-religious and missionary overtones. And like the Communists they posed as a movement of youth and developed an extraordinarily high degree of activism. Their divergent national traditions notwithstanding, fascist ideologies also display many similarities. They all tended to look back to a national past of heroism and greatness; they proclaimed a new simplicity of morals and cultural life; they advocated a national-ist and social renewal. All these aims were combined with a pledge fanatically to fight international socialism and Marxism and with a deep disdain for political liberalism and for par-liamentary democracy which was to be replaced by a new elite cult and authoritarian principles of education based on the notions of leadership and subordination. An important differ-ence between Italian Fascism (and fascist movements such as the Spanish *Falange*) on the one hand and Nazism (and fascist movements in East Central Europe) on the other was that the former, unlike the latter, gave only little emphasis to anti-Semitism and racism. But essentially there are historical and national–cultural reasons for this difference.

Ideologically fascism was prefigured in certain types of pre-1914 integral nationalism, represented in Germany above all by Pan-German and *völkische* currents. Its novelty which the First World War had promoted consisted primarily in its capacity to attract mass support and in its public appearance which was no longer merely wedded to the propagation of ideology, but advocated physical struggle and activism. That the political climate in Germany had undergone a radical shift, is also re-flected in the more widespread preparedness to incorporate anti-Semitic principles into the constitutions of clubs and associ-ations. The educated and 'proper' notables who had run these clubs in the Wilhelmine period had still resisted such tend-encies. *Völkisch*-anti-Semitic parties and groups, which dated back to the pre-1914 period, had then merely existed on the margins of politics and society. Their role was relatively minor and hardly more significant than French anti-Semitism which had burst forth in the 1890s during the Dreyfus Affair. It was certainly much weaker than the Pan-Slavic anti-Semitism of the pogroms in Tsarist Russia. Change came in this respect during the First World War when East European Jews fled westward from the army-occupied territories of Poland, the Baltic provinces and the Ukraine and, above all, when the Fatherland Party, which had been formed in 1917, started its propaganda campaigns. It was from these quarters that a purposeful attempt was made to divert a growing dissatisfaction with the monarchy and the government onto 'Jewish' war-profiteers and shirkers.

However, after 1918 it was the prominence of a number of Jews on the revolutionary Left, among the Spartacists and on the left wing of the Independent Socialists which gave a massive boost to anti-Semitism. Thus the short-lived Soviet Republic in Munich in the spring of 1919 was grist to the mills of the anti-Semites on the nationalist Right who skilfully linked these resentments to the *Dolchstosslegende*. Left-wing 'Jewish' revolutionaries and 'traitors', on Moscow's pay-roll, were alleged to have unleashed strike movements in the final phases of the war; they were said to have stabbed the army, which had not been vanquished in the field, in the back and to have forced the abdication of the monarch. In the autumn of 1919 no lesser man than the former Field Marshal Hindenburg forcefully promoted this view in his statement before a Reichstag Committee of Investigation. But already in the spring of 1919, after the Allies had handed down their humiliating peace terms at Versailles, *völkische* and anti-Semitic clubs had begun to mushroom all over the country. The history of the *Deutschvölkischer Schutz- und Trutzbund*, which Uwe Lohalm has written, comes to mind as one example. At about the same time the Pan-German League or the *Hochschulring* of *völkische* student groups introduced a clause into their constitutions barring Jews from membership. Anti-Semitism now became the motive behind a radical agitation against well-known representatives of republican politics and above all behind an activist terrorism. Walther Rathenau, the Foreign Minister, became its most prominent victim when he was murdered in 1922. It is difficult to measure the extent of anti-Semitic ideas and attitudes in the early postwar years because the *völkische* and anti-Semitic associations were so fragmented. But if compared with the pre-1914 period, the strength of the movement had evidently increased and a qualitative shift had taken place. Perhaps even more important was the fact that traces of this type of anti-Semitism kept spreading throughout the entire right of the political spectrum, and could be found not least in the pamphlets and journals of a variety of national-revolutionary and Young Conservative groups which were now emerging. Their activities have been described from different perspectives by Armin Mohler and Kurt Sontheimer.

The war also caused major changes and upheavals among the victorious nations. But they found it easier to contain them psychologically and politically and to channel them into reform-ist strategies. The electoral reform in Britain and the transform-ation of the Empire into the Commonwealth may be cited as telling examples here. The main losers of the First World War (Germany, Austria-Hungary, Russia) on the other hand experi-enced the collapse of their monarchical systems as a direct consequence of defeat; this the more so since the Western Allies, particularly after the American entry in 1917, had conducted this war increasingly as an ideological campaign aiming at the libera-tion of the smaller nations from the yoke of autocratic militar-ism. In the case of Germany, the US President, Wilson, had linked the peace terms to an abdication of the Kaiser. If nothing else, it was this connection which subsequently caused the Republic, which had emerged from the defeat, to be derided as a dishonourable concession to the victors and as a 'betrayal' of the nation.

Many Germans quickly forgot the grievances which they had felt towards the monarchy in the final years of the war. They also struck from their memory the fury which had surfaced in Oc-tober 1918 when it became clear that the Kaiser and the High Command had misled the population up to the summer of that year into believing that victory was just around the corner. At that time General Erich Ludendorff, Germany's virtual dictator, had demanded, out of the blue, the immediate conclusion of an armistice to be negotiated by the new Reich Chancellor, Prince Max von Baden, if a military catastrophe in the West was to be avoided. The Hohenzollern monarchy and the monarchical sys-tems in the German states would not have collapsed so quickly in November 1918 had it not been for these elemental moods of popular fury combined with the widespread view that the Kaiser and the old regime had thoroughly failed. Nor would it have been possible for the Social Democrats, who had been included in the move towards parliamentary government of October 1918, to take over from the monarchy as smoothly as they did under the leadership of Friedrich Ebert.

But the old forces of conservatism found themselves in a state of exhaustion only briefly during the phase of an immediate threat of a Spartacist revolution in 1918/19. It was this peculiar situation which had temporarily given such a boost to the moderate Left and the parties of the middle-ground (Social Democrats, Democrats and Catholic Centre Party) that they had gained over 70 per cent of the total vote in the elections for the National Assembly in January 1919. But this strong popular support dwindled quickly after the imposition of the Versailles Treaty and its ratification on 1 January 1920. The Kapp Putsch of March 1920 was the first signal for the mobilisation of the counter-revolution although the coup itself was amateurishly and insufficiently prepared and hence doomed to failure. The Reichstag elections of June 1920 then demonstrated clearly how far the balance of political forces had shifted to the Right or, to some extent, also to the extreme Left in comparison with the January 1919 poll. Thenceforth the so-called Weimar coalition no longer held the majority.

The harsh peace of Versailles was psychologically unaccept-able above all to the patriotically inclined German middle clas-ses. It constrasted too sharply with the exuberant nationalist and imperialist expectations which these groups had cherished over many years. From the 1880s onwards the German elites and large sections of the bourgeoisie had taken a keen interest in the country's ambitions to become a world power. These ambi-tions had found expression in the colonial and naval policies of the Kaiser and later during the Boxer Rebellion in China and the 1905 Moroccan Crisis in which passions had been aroused by the nationalist press. Germany's power-political aspirations and economic expansionist interests had turned towards Africa and the Far East as well as the Middle East via the Balkans and the Baghdad Railway project. Bismarck had still pursued a cautious policy of consolidating the position of the new German Empire through alliances. But with Germany's military and economic power growing, this strategy had increasingly been substituted under William II by a policy of imperialist risk-taking. It was a policy which was even prepared to include in its calculations a violent destruction of the limits which Britain and France, above all, had set to Wilhelmine power politics. It was against the background of such traditions that the German leadership consciously risked a war against the Western Allies. Nor did the country's military and political leaders abandon their dogmatic adherence to the imperialist war aims which had been drawn up soon after the outbreak of the First World War. This inflexibility remained unchanged even when it became clear that, following initial successes, the campaign in the West had turned into a long-drawn-out war of attrition. It would have been possible at that point to win a peace on the basis of the *status quo ante*. Instead the Reich leadership provoked the entry into the war of the United States and hence a decisive reinforcement of the Allied war effort by embarking upon 'unlimited' submarine warfare, even though it was useless as strategy for bringing Britain to her knees. Nor did these realities prevent the government, prodded by the High Command, from exploiting the opportunities which presented themselves after the collapse of Russia in 1917. With the Treaty of Brest-Litovsk Germany showed no political qualms about establishing a hegemonic position which reached far into Eastern Europe and the Ukraine. This move counteracted and discredited the demands by the parties of the left and the centre (Social Democrats, Progressives and Catholic Centre Party) to conclude a peace without annexations.

It is against the background of these far-reaching ambitions which many Germans continued to hold up to the summer of 1918 that the shock of the Versailles peace terms must be seen. In contradistinction to what the Germans felt in 1945, many of them had not stopped dreaming of national greatness in 1918. If the legend of the stab in the back found so much support, it was because nationalist energies were still strong and far from being exhausted. It was for the same reason that many ex-soldiers, but even leading Social Democrats, whom the war had emotionally integrated into the fatherland, reacted to the defeat and to the Versailles Treaty with incredulity. Indignation was widespread and a basic attitude of resistance emerged. There was a strong determination not to accept the 'shame of Versailles', but to undo it by whatever means.

However, perhaps the most fateful consequence of the Versailles Treaty was that from 1919 onwards it largely blocked all self-criticism of prewar Wilhelmine imperialism and of the monarchy's wartime record. The critique of the Treaty which all parties engaged in created something like a new artificial *Burgfrieden* in the sphere of German foreign policy. Aspirations were geared above all to an early revision of the Treaty. The repercussions of this posture upon domestic politics and the general political climate were considerable and in many ways it also had a corrosive effect on the stability and credibility of the Weimar Republic as a whole.

In subsequent years the moderate republican forces invariably found themselves psychologically and propagandistically in a weaker position within this common anti-Versailles front. This was ultimately also true of Foreign Minister Gustav Stresemann who had undergone a conversion from the hardline annexationist he had been during the war to an adherent of *Realpolitik*. In 1925 he negotiated the Locarno Pact which recognised the territorial status quo in the West and hence parts of the Versailles Treaty. Time and again the moderates were pushed into alliances with the nationalists on the Right or had to tolerate their hardline revisionism. The aid given to right-wing Free Corps and border protection units during the plebiscites especially in Upper Silesia in 1920–1 may serve as an example here. Even Social Democratic politicians were involved in this support. There also occurred the breaches of the disarmament clauses of the Versailles Treaty, actively promoted as they were by the *Reichswehr*, resulting in the establishment of local militias and other 'Black *Reichswehr*' contingents as well as the build-up of arms caches. A third example is the secret co-operation with the Red Army which began even before the Rapallo Pact of 1922. Aided and abetted by democratic forces, the Weimar Republic developed illegal structures of nationalist resistance which became intertwined with the official organs of the state in quite problematical ways. This was particularly true of the *Reichswehr*. As a result, the militant forces on the nationalist Right were given quasi-governmental auxiliary functions, and this in turn made it extraordinarily difficult to combat these same radicals with the help of the police or the courts when they challenged the republican constitution and the domestic peace. Small wonder that the Weimar judiciary frequently turned a blind eye to right-wing activities, if political terrorists were to be prosecuted. The problem was that such terrorists could often pretend to pursue 'idealistic' patriotic objectives when, for example, they waged their underground war against Rhenish 'separatists' or, in 1923, against the French and their German 'sympathisers' during the Ruhr Occupation. This schizophrenia which furthered double standards of morality and a split system spread like poison and undermined the constitutional substance of the existing political system. As a consequence many authorities and politicians found themselves on the downward slope well before 1933 when they trivialised, exculpated or amnestied serious political crimes.

To these psychological and ideological preconditions of radical nationalism must be added other weighty factors, above all the postwar economic crisis and, from the summer of 1922 onwards, galloping inflation. For the most part, hyperinflation was a result of the massive debts which the Reich had accumulated during the war and of the inflationary financial policies adopted by the public sector in the early postwar years. Only to a small extent was it a consequence of the reparations burdens imposed by the Versailles Treaty. And yet this psychologically pernicious link between reparations and the country's depressed economic state turned reparations into the main target of the right-wing opposition. The crises of 1922–3 and 1929–30 which had overwhelmingly quite different roots could thus be distorted very persuasively into an enslavement, through reparations, of Germany perpetrated by the 'plutocratic' Western allies. Whenever a republican government made an attempt to find, in negotiation with the West, a pragmatic solution to the problem and to achieve a reduction of reparations payments, it was immediately attacked as a stooge of the victors and an agent of an infamous 'policy of fulfillment'.

In this way the National Opposition was able to mobilise people against international plans aiming at a solution of the reparations question — first against the Dawes Plan of 1924 and later against the Young Plan of 1929–30. However, this agitation succeeded only because large sections of the population had in fact suffered serious economic and social setbacks either through the inflation or through the renewed agricultural crisis and ultimately through the 'Great Slump'. The significance of the 'Great Inflation' which accompanied the early years of the Republic and the psychological impact it had upon attitudes towards the postwar political system can hardly be overestimated. Thus many members of the lower middle classes who saw their savings or their inherited wealth being eaten up by hyperinflation, government inaction in the face of this revolutionary devaluation of the currency was tantamount to a policy of expropriation by the state. They regarded it as a massive fraud perpetrated by the state against its citizens.

However, there were also other reasons, if the Weimar Republic failed to retain middle-class support. To some extent middle-class rejection was based on the same considerations which, mirror-like, led the Social Democrats and trade unions to give such solid support to the Republic. Thus the welfare state provided a tangible improvement for the industrial labour force in comparison with the prewar period. It introduced collective bargaining, work place participation and the 48-hour week. There were also better wages in which the state had a hand by acting as a mediator in wage conflicts and by being empowered to impose arbitrations upon the two sides of industry, usually upon the employers. The Weimar welfare state which the unions wanted to uphold was perceived by many middle-class people as a hostile 'state of the trade unions'. They attacked it not merely because wage and income differentials had been reduced in favour of the working class, but also because other barriers which had limited the influence of labour in Imperial Germany had been removed. In particular this was true of the restricted suffrage systems in the states and local councils.

In the 'good old days' of the Empire, large sections of the bourgeoisie had become used to viewing the organised working class as an inferior group and subculture. Consequently they now saw it as historically illegitimate that the labour movement had gained a considerable share in the political and social power structure within the framework of Weimar's parliamentary democracy by virtue of its organisational and electoral strength. And this antagonism in turn unleashed massive bourgeois aversions against the existing constitutional order. The traditional disdain for the lower classes was also an important source of the passionate hatred which Ebert, the former trade unionist and journeyman saddler, encountered as President of the Republic among the conservative upper classes and among the bourgeoisie until his death in 1925. The notion which the right-wing opposition had invented that the Republic whose colours were black, red and golden, had been created and was dominated by the (red) Marxist, the (golden) Jewish–capitalist and the (black) clerical–Catholic Internationals, represented a prejudice which could be quickly mobilised in times of economic crisis. The fact that the Republic which had been founded at a time of national and social decline remained unglamorous and saddled with great problems meant that its parliamentary structure also failed to attract the support of wide circles. Worse, for many Germans it became an object of hatred, especially in times of crisis. Their 'flight into hatred' (Eva Reichmann) provided them with psychological compensation, and no one else reflected these sentiments more intensely and momentously than Hitler with his Nazi movement.

2.2. *Hitler and the NSDAP during the Period of Stabilisation, 1924–1928*

During the early critical years of the Weimar Republic up to 1923, the Nazi Party and other right-wing nationalist forces had at times reached dangerous strength. Nevertheless, its attempts to destroy the Republic had failed. After the Kapp Putsch of March 1920 came the collapse of the 'Black *Reichswehr*' uprising at Küstrin in October 1923, followed six weeks later by the abortive Hitler Putsch in Munich. If the Republic succeeded in asserting itself against these coups, this was also due to the fact that it had to defend itself against revolutionary movements on both Right and Left. The result of this apparent paradox was that the main pillar of the Republic, the SPD, was able to retain a relatively strong position in this period. Moreover, the threat of violent revolution also forced the army back into the old pact which Ebert and General Groener had concluded in November 1918 for the purpose of securing the existing order against the threat posed by the extreme Left.

On the other hand, the course of events in 1918–19 enabled the army to retain a position outside the republican structure. At the time of the Kapp Putsch its leaders left no doubt that they were not prepared to move against those officers and men from their own ranks who had supported the coup. As General Hans von Seeckt put it at the time: *'Reichswehr* does not shoot upon *Reichswehr!'*. It was also evident then as well as later how problematical was the posture of neutrality which the army leadership observed *vis-à-vis* the Republic. After all, this neutrality was not precisely tantamount to loyalty and realiability; rather it strongly promoted ideas which aimed at the restoration of the Hohenzollern monarchy or other authoritarian forms of government. And yet the army was not prepared formally to breach the Constitution and hence remained faithful to its traditional self-image as the conservative guardian of the constitutional *status quo.* Even Hitler in Bavaria did not succeed in drawing the army into his camp, and Seeckt significantly did not use the powers which he gained in November 1923 after the proclamation of the national emergency in order to establish a military dictatorship, much to the disappointment of the Right. Contrary to the fears of the Left, he remained loyal to the Constitution.

Once the threat from the extreme Left (in Saxony and Thuringia) and from the Right (in Bavaria) had been removed, the Republic began to move towards a new stability and phase of normalisation. One week after the defeat of the Hitler Putsch, on 15 November 1923, a new currency, the *Rentenmark*, was issued, initiating the successful solution to the problem of inflation. These monetary policies were accompanied in the winter of 1923–4 by a series of emergency decrees relating to social and economic affairs. These decrees were based on an enabling act, passed by the Reichstag with the help of the SPD, which, for the next three months, gave the Stresemann Cabinet full powers to enact legislation. Among this legislation was the Revaluation Act of 14 February 1924 which compensated mortgage creditors for a small part of their losses (15 per cent). However, this measure did little to mollify those who had lost most of their savings in the Great Inflation of 1923.

Another consequence of the currency reform was that it increased unemployment which, together with the growing conflict over the Dawes Plan reparations proposals, once more furthered radical tendencies on the Right and on the Left. The extreme Right obtained 26 per cent of the votes in the national elections of 4 May 1924 (DNVP: 19.5 per cent; Nazis and *Völkische*: 6.5 per cent). The Communists whose share had dwindled in the early 1920s gained 12.6 per cent. But when fresh elections were called a few months later, on 7 December 1924, the tide had begun to change. The economic recovery had set in. The more moderate sections of the DNVP were more prepared to support Stresemann's diplomatic strategy. The stabilisation had been initiated, but the governmental balance of power had moved away from the SPD towards the moderate middle-class parties. The results of the December poll confirmed this trend. The *Völkische* obtained a mere 3 per cent; the Communist vote dropped to 9 per cent.

Aided by foreign and particularly by American loans, the industrial economy of Germany regained its momentum. The expansion was characterised by rationalisation, the introduction of new technologies and by concentration. There was a boom in the construction of public and communal buildings and amenities, especially in the big cities. Unemployment benefit schemes and labour courts were introduced, reinforcing the 'welfare net'. Another feature of this period was an extraordinarily rich cultural life, particularly in Berlin. With the signing of the Locarno Pact in 1925 and the acceptance of Germany as a member of the League of Nations there began a policy of reconciliation with the country's former enemies and with it a real prospect of a further modification of the most pressing clauses of the Versailles Treaty, i.e. reparations, the regaining of territorial sovereignty in the Rhine-Ruhr region and military equality.

It looked as if in these circumstances the majority of the German middle classes might slowly get used to parliamentary democracy for which they had hitherto shown so little affection. A revolution from the Left seemed unlikely. In national and provincial elections between 1924 and 1928–9, the Communist vote had begun to level out around the 10 per cent mark. Following the death of Lenin, the *Komintern* (Communist International) abandoned its earlier policy of immediate revolutionary action in favour of a long-term strategy aimed at mass agitation in preparation of a revolution. Nor was there an immediate threat from the radical Right. Mussolini's seizure of power appeared to most German observers, even in the nationalist camp, to be a special case. It was not thought to be able to serve as a model and had little attraction for Germany. Moreover the Fascist government in Rome had stepped up its policy of Italianisation in South Tyrol. It also promoted the independence of Austria which was anathema to the Pan-Germanism prevailing on the German Right.

The failure of the radical right-wing opposition up to 1923–4 was to no small degree a consequence of its organisational and political disunity. This disunity had surfaced again even within the bloc of radical paramilitary associations which had been allied with the NSDAP in Bavaria in the months before the Hitler Putsch. The collapse of this coup and the subsequent ban on the Nazi Party and the SA promoted further fragmention. In Munich and South Germany there emerged, as a Nazi successor organisation, the so-called *Grossdeutsche Volksgemeinschaft*, led by Alfred Rosenberg, Julius Streicher and Hermann Esser. Meanwhile in the North, Nazis and *Völkische* combined to form the *Nationalsozialistische Freiheitsbewegung* under the joint 'Reich leadership' of Erich Ludendorff, Gregor Strasser and Albrecht von Graefe, once head of the *Deutschvölkische Freiheitspartei* which had likewise been outlawed after 1923.

Hitler, having been given a prison term on 1 April 1924, for his putschist activities, had been sent to Landsberg prison. However, the prison authorities treated him very generously and he was allowed to receive fellow Nazis for talks. At first he tried to influence the 'movement' from his cell. But from the summer of 1924 he refrained from such interventions, probably also in order to demonstrate his indispensability and to retain his authority for the time after his release from Landsberg. Meanwhile he upheld his claim to leadership among his Nazi fellow-prisoners. Apart from Hermann Kriebel and Friedrich Weber, he was temporarily surrounded by up to forty former putschists, many of whom had been members of the *Stosstrupp Hitler*. Among them was Rudolf Hess, who formally took over the post of 'Secretary to the *Führer*', and Emil Maurice, who acted as a sort of valet to Hitler.

The composition of a major programmatic statement, later entitled *Mein Kampf*, which Hitler started in the summer of 1924 was seen by him as a means of buttressing his leadership role. The first volume with the working title *Four Years of Struggle against Lies, Stupidity and Cowardice* was completed in Landsberg prison and published in the following year. Two years later, in 1927, Hitler brought out the second part. Editorial improvements in which Father Stempfle, the editor of the anti-Semitic *Miesbacher Anzeiger*, also had a hand failed to transform the manuscript's basic character: it read like Hitler's spoken words, typified by the verbose monologue-style of his speeches. All attempts at providing a systematic analysis did not prevent extensive repetitions. It thus always proved a strain to read the book from cover to cover.

Especially the autobiographical parts of *Mein Kampf* and the sections dealing with a justification of his earlier political actions frequently make it impossible to separate authenticity from self-stylisation. Nevertheless, those parts of the 800-page book which deal with Hitler's political and ideological views are unusually frank and telling. Despite this frankness, with one exception, only stylistic and no substantial changes, were made to the many later editions. The book sold 287,000 copies up to 30 January 1933; subsequently around 10 million copies were in circulation.

In the penultimate chapter of the first volume entitled '*Volk and Race*', Hitler extensively unfolded, in his fantastic and stubborn mode of discourse, the racist foundations of his entire *Weltanschauung*. The hundreds of race-theoretical, anti-Semitic and Social-Darwinist pamphlets which he had read in his adolescence in Vienna were combined here with a pseudo-systematic dogmatism into a cosmology of the eternal struggle of the Aryan who creates culture versus the Jew who is said to undermine the cultural and racial substance of the former. And all this was put together with no less superficially imbibed notions concerning the 'iron laws' of nature and of human history which were allegedly dominated by the 'eternal struggle of the species. It is the superior races that would assert themselves; subjugation was the fate of the inferior species. Here we find statements like these:

The stronger must dominate and not blend with the weaker, thus sacrificing his own greatness. Only the born weakling can view this as cruel, but he after all is only a weak and limited man . . . And struggle is always a means for improving a species' health and power of resistance and, therefore, a cause of its higher development . . . All great cultures of the past perished only because the originally creative race died out from blood-poisoning.[1]

To Hitler, the Aryans were the only 'race of genius' which alone was motivated by 'idealism'. They were opposed by the Jews, the embodiment of exploitation and decomposition. It is at this point that Hitler deviated from his often consciously adopted style of sober pseudo-scientific analysis. His rhetoric is permeated by blind hatred and reveals a grotesque obsession with the alleged poisoning of German blood and humanity by the Jews:

With satanic joy in his face, the black-haired Jewish youth lurks in wait for the unsuspecting girl whom he defiles with his blood, thus stealing her from her people. With every means he tries to destroy the racial foundations of the people he has set out to subjugate. Just as he himself systematically ruins women and girls, he does not shrink back from pulling down the blood barriers for others, even on a large scale. It was and it is Jews who bring the Negroes into the Rhineland, always with the same secret thought and clear aim of ruining the hated white race by the necessarily resulting bastardisation, throwing it down from its cultural and political height, and himself rising to be its master.[2]
. . . . Culturally he contaminates art, literature, the theatre, makes a mockery of natural feeling, overthrows all concepts of beauty and sublimity, of the noble and the good, and instead drags men down into the sphere of his own base nature.[3]

Hitler added that for centuries the Jews had exploited the 'host societies' economically. Later they invented the internationalism of Freemasonry, pacificism and parliamentary democracy as means towards the same end. But finally they deployed the most pernicious instrument of national decomposition: Marxism. In his view, Germany's collapse in the First World War was likewise caused by the neglect of the race question:

1. A. Hitler, *Mein Kampf* (transl. by R. Manheim), London 1969, pp. 259, 262.
2. Ibid., p. 295.
3. Ibid., p. 296.

The defeats on the battlefield in August, 1918, would have been child's play to bear. They stood in no proportion to the victories of our people. It was not they that caused our downfall; no, it was brought about by that power which prepared these defeats by systematically over many decades robbing our people of the political and moral instincts and forces which alone make nations capable and hence worthy of existence.[4]

The second volume of *Mein Kampf* then pin-pointed another axiomatic idea in Hitler's *Weltanschauung*: large-scale expansion towards the East as a means of gaining the territorial base for an empire dominated by the German master race. It was a plan which went far beyond the confines of a nationalist policy of revisionism touted by the Right. As Hitler explained:

Germany will either be a world power or there will be no Germany. And for world power she needs that magnitude which will give her the position she needs in the present period, and life to her citizens. And so we National Socialists consciously draw a line beneath the foreign policy tendency of our pre-War period. We take up where we broke off six hundred years ago. We stop the endless German movement to the south and west, and turn our gaze towards the land in the east. At long last we break off the colonial and commercial policy of the pre-War period and shift to the soil policy of the future.[5]

The second volume also contains a justification of Hitler's fixation about 'living space' which was directed against the Soviet Union. These passages provide an insight into what, in the final analysis, motivated him in developing this fixation. At first glance there existed seemingly sober alliance considerations: given the European power constellation which had resulted from the First World War, Germany, he argued, could hope to counter France's hegemonic position in Europe only in conjunction with Britain and Italy. An alliance with Soviet Russia was deemed far too risky by him, if only because of the Bolshevik menace. At this point it was racist and ideological considerations which appeared for the first time in Hitler's foreign policy thinking and began to gain the decisive weight. Owing to the rule of 'Jewish Bolshevism' Russia was on its way

4. Ibid.
5. Ibid., pp. 598f.

to losing its fibre which held it together as a nation-state. As he put it:

> For centuries Russia drew nourishment from this Germanic nucleus of its upper leading strata. Today it can be regarded as almost totally exterminated and extinguished. It has been replaced by the Jew. Impossible as it is for the Russian by himself to shake off the yoke of the Jew by his own resources, it is equally impossible for the Jew to maintain the mighty empire forever. He himself is no element of organisation, but a ferment of decomposition.[6]

The fact that Hitler was able to justify his new foreign policy objectives in racial terms now transformed them into an *idée fixe*. In another section of *Mein Kampf* Hitler dwelt at length on the importance of firmly adhering to certain ideas and programmatic statements, even if they were wrong. Only in this way would it be possible to give the Nazi 'movement' steadiness and a clear vision of its objectives. This argument also applied to the *idées fixes* of Hitler's *Weltanschauung* in a broader sense. What helped him in this was his self-hypnotic capacity to combine politically desirable 'grand' designs and adversary images with a fanatical belief in his ideological vision legitimating his objectives. It was this same capacity which later resulted in a complete loss of his ability to align his decisions with political reality when he proceeded, after the beginning of the Second World War, to put his transpolitical visions into practice. No other Nazi leader had a similarly strongly developed capacity like Hitler. It formed the basis of the unwavering certainty with which he pursued his policies; it instilled him with his belief in himself and in his mission; it informed the messianic style of his public appearances and speeches; it enabled him to become the missionary creator and *Führer* of the Nazi movement, even if, for some considerable time after his release from Landsberg prison in December 1924, he had to leave the reorganisation of the party to others.

After the failure of the Putsch and the composition of the first part of *Mein Kampf* Hitler had definitely abandoned the notion of being no more than the drummer (*Trommler*) of the nationalist movement. His first political decisions after his release reveal a

6. Ibid.

determination to lead and dominate personally which was clearly stronger than before his trial. At the beginning of January 1925 he had a conversation with Heinrich Held, the Bavarian Minister-President. In it he pledged that in future he would pursue politics by legal means alone. He dissociated himself from the *völkische* anti-Christianism into which Ludendorff had lapsed increasingly under the influence of his wife Mathilde.

Reassured by this conversation and under the impression of the decline of the *völkische* vote in the elections of December 1924, the Bavarian government rescinded the ban on the NSDAP and its newspaper, the *Völkischer Beobachter*. Subsequently Hitler called on his former supporters to meet for the refounding of the old party on 26 February 1925 in the Munich *Bürgerbräukeller*, the place of its defeat of November 1923. In the course of this meeting he succeeded with surprising speed in uniting the various splinter groups by categorically upholding his claim to sole leadership. Those *völkische* groups which were not prepared to subordinate themselves in this way had stayed away. Gregor Strasser, too, detached himself from Graefe and Ludendorff and put the following which he had meanwhile gathered together in North and West Germany at the disposal of the newly founded NSDAP.

Two months later Röhm, who was not prepared to subordinate himself to Hitler unconditionally, left the fold and subsequently went to Bolivia as a military adviser. He had created a substitute for the banned SA in the shape of the *Frontbann* which was conceived as a paramilitary association without party affiliation. Following the disaster of 1923, Hitler was totally opposed to a refounding of the SA. Henceforth SA groups merely existed at *Gau* level without a central leadership and loosely attached to the local Nazi Party. It took another eighteen months for Hitler to nominate, on 1 November 1926, a leader for the entire SA organisation. This was Franz von Pfeffer, a retired captain and hitherto a *Gauleiter* in the Ruhr district. Pfeffer also took charge of the *Schutzstaffel* (SS) which had emerged from the *Stosstrupp Hitler*. It was a special formation which was deliberately kept small and designed to provide personal protection for the top Nazi leadership. Its hallmarks were a black cap with a death's head badge and a brown shirt with black tie. Finally Pfeffer had the Hitler Youth (HJ), established in 1926, subordinated to him.

In order to obviate the threat of a completely decentralised SA which was removed from the top leadership and might engage in a renewed putschist separatism, Hitler granted Pfeffer independence in organisational terms. But he insisted that he remained under the political suzerainty and uniform discipline of the NSDAP and its *Führer*, Hitler. Pfeffer and his successor Röhm who returned in 1930 to become SA *Stabschef* introduced strict discipline, military hierarchies and organisational structures into the SA as well as drill, athletics and small arms practice. But there were narrow and deliberately maintained limits to these structures and activities. They cut across the *bündische* structures which the lower echelons in particular had taken over from the tradition of the Free Corps and paramilitary associations of the early postwar years. These latter structures were geared to the idea of comrades grouped around a local *Führer*, and the egalitarian principle that an 'SA man is an SA man'. These special ties were indispensable if the dynamic preparedness for activism and sacrifice of the mostly young SA members was to be retained. Thus military discipline and obedience of the individual SA man towards his superior became intertwined with the mostly more important principle of unconditional personal 'loyalty' and comradeship. The formal sanctions which SA leaders were able to impose on unruly men could be given much greater force through informal methods of ostracism, ranging from 'defamation' (*Verfemung*) to night-time mugging and murder, with which 'disloyal' comrades were threatened. It was also characteristic that ideological and political training was virtually non-existent in the SA. The *Ten Commandments of the SA Man* which the SA leadership issued in 1927 were simply called *Doctrine Concerning the Liberation of the German People*.[7] The loyalty that was expected was geared, above all, to the *Führer*, and 'Guide of the [Nazi] Idea', Adolf Hitler. At the annual party rally SA contingents were given their ritual consecration by Hitler. They were surrounded by selected carriers of Nazi banners which included the 'blood banner' of 9 November 1923, the day of the Hitler Putsch. These occasions were designed to renew the mutual vow of loyalty. On the other hand,

---

7. W. Horn, *Der Marsch zur Machtergreifung*, Königstein 1980, p. 293. See also P.H. Merkl, *The Making of a Stormtrooper*, Princeton 1980.

it was precisely this *bündische* aspect of the SA, its sympathies with the left wing of the NSDAP and its 'socialism' as well as its organisational independence which bore the seeds of future conflict between the party and its paramilitary arm. The Stennes Revolt in Berlin was one expression of this. These tensions were all the more bound to arise since Pfeffer overwhelmingly put former Free Corps officers into higher command positions. Among them were a number of aristocrats like Manfred von Killinger, the Saxon regional leader, Curt von Ulrich and Werner von Fichte whose home base was in the Rhineland.

Nor did the Nazi Party at first develop in a manner which indicated clear direction by Hitler and the Munich headquarters. In practice Hitler was able to assert himself only with great difficulty. There was considerable resistance to him and violations of the party rules had to be treated with great leniency. Only in this way did it prove possible for the central office which had been established in the summer of 1925 under Philipp Bouhler as general secretary, Franz Xaver Schwarz as treasurer and Max Amann, the director of the Eher-Verlag publishing house, to gain recognition from regional and local groups, many of which had been founded independently. Local groups were also reluctant to transfer to the headquarter its share of the membership dues. They were slow in reporting membership gains and losses or in asking for confirmation of new leaders. It was typical of this early phase when hierarchies and the *Führer* principle were far from firmly established throughout the organisation that local and regional leaders were in most cases still being elected. Only from 1928 onwards, when the organisation began to be streamlined, did the principle of nomination from above become the basic pattern. It was to this change that the only tangible alteration to the text of *Mein Kampf* referred. The editions up to 1928 had contained a statement that the Nazi movement adhered to the notion of 'Germanic democracy' combined with the electoral principle of the leader who enjoyed unconditional authority once elected. From 1930 onwards, editions merely referred to the 'principle of unconditional *Führer* authority twinned with the highest responsibility'.[8]

8. H. Hammer, 'Die deutschen Ausgaben von Hitlers "Mein Kampf"', in *Vierteljahrshefte für Zeitgeschichte*, 4/1956, pp. 171f.

Until 1927 Hitler moreover suffered from the handicap that the Bavarian government had barred him from making public speeches. Most other state governments followed the Bavarian lead after Hitler's demeanour at the founding meeting on 26 February 1925 had raised serious doubts about the sincerity of his earlier promise to pursue his policies only by legal means. In 1925–6 Hitler therefore largely withdrew from party work. He spoke only occasionally before private meetings or wrote articles for the *Völkische Beobachter* or the party-owned *Illustrierter Beobachter*. For the rest of the time, he resumed his earlier life style as a bohemian in politics. He surrounded himself with devout companions from Munich, wealthy patrons of the Nazi cause or new admirers, like Heinrich Hoffmann, his later 'personal photographer'. He hung out in the *Osteria Bavaria*, *Café Neumaier* or the rented country house at the top of the Obersalzberg near Garmisch-Partenkirchen. The daily routine of party organisation and agitation was largely left to other leaders.

It was against this background that Gregor Strasser, the *Gauleiter* for Lower Bavaria, was able to strengthen his position from 1925 onwards. In the previous year, he had gained a seat in the Reichstag, and in 1927–8 he became head of the central organisation and propaganda departments. Hitler also left to Strasser the reorganisation of the North and West German NSDAP which the latter had begun before 1925. Strasser was very tall, basically 'straight' and personally well regarded by his collaborators. He had a natural talent for politics and political organisation and was generally very different from Hitler. Through his father, a royal-Bavarian civil servant, he had been exposed to Christian-social ideas. In 1918 he returned from the war having risen to the position of *Oberleutnant*. A year later he completed his pharmaceutical studies which he had begun before joining the army. He got married and acquired a profitable pharmacy in the Lower Bavarian town of Landshut. Strasser was not the type of member, frequently to be encountered in the Nazi Party, who had been 'uprooted' by the war and the postwar crisis. He was not a Hitler follower who had been politicised and radicalised from a sense of social insecurity. However, together with his younger brother Otto, then a student at Munich University, he volunteered for the Free Corps Epp and participated in the destruction of the short-lived Bavarian Soviet Republic. This experience moved him into the orbit of the Bavarian paramilitary associations. He himself founded such an association at Landshut. He came into contact with Ludendorff and Hitler. In 1922 he put himself and his Landshut contingent at Hitler's disposal. Soon he had become SA leader and Nazi *Gauleiter* for Lower Bavaria.

Otto Strasser was more of an intellectual but less sturdy. What united the two brothers were their adherence to vague *völkische* ideas and their social and national-revolutionary convictions. Gregor harboured considerable qualms about Hitler. But his feelings of personal loyalty prevented him from challenging Hitler's leadership until 1932, although he was one of the best Nazi speakers. He was also a more circumspect, more practical and personally more reliable organiser than the *Führer* himself. Nevertheless, like Röhm, he recognised without envy the superior visionary and compulsively rhetorical capabilities of Hitler and this, time and again, persuaded him to hold back with whatever criticism he had.

It was due to Strasser's relentless efforts that the party, which at the beginning of 1925 had no more than a few thousand members, made good progress organisationally. The general political constellation of the mid-1920s was not favourable to such efforts, but his untiring agitation was rewarded. In 1925 he himself spoke at some one hundred party meetings. By the end of that year, the NSDAP had regained around 27,000 inscribed members. Up to the end of 1928 this figure had risen to 108,000 and the number of local groups had multiplied. Considering that at this time few people actually voted for the party, the organisational network which spanned the whole of Germany was remarkably dense, even if it is true that initially it remained confined to towns and cities.

In 1924, during the period of mass unemployment, Strasser and a number of younger activists, among them Joseph Goebbels in Elberfeld and the later *Gauleiter* Karl Kaufmann, Erich Koch and Josef Wagner in the Ruhr area, began their campaign in north-west Germany. This explains why an explicitly 'revolutionary' brand of Nazism emerged in these working-class regions, promoted by an *Arbeitsgemeinschaft* of the north-west German party organisations which Strasser had formed in 1925. Nationalist resentments against the French occupation of the

Rhineland and the Ruhr area provided a fertile soil for a national-revolutionary approach. The establishment of the Kampf-Verlag in Berlin which published, *inter alia*, *Der nationale Sozialist*, a journal edited by Otto Strasser, must also be seen in this context. In 1925–6 Otto Strasser and also Goebbels found ideas about a German nation of proletarians who were being exploited by the capitalist West much more appealing than Hitler's perspective who at this time was in the process of formulating his anti-Communist doctrine of expansion towards the East. The struggle against the French occupation of the Ruhr had done much to promote such 'national–Bolshevik' interpretations which, in 1923 and influenced by Karl Radek, had also inspired parts of the Communists. Moreover, in the winter of 1925–6 there arose a particular point of conflict between the Nazi 'Left' and the Munich headquarters. This was the plebiscite, initiated by the Communists, but also supported by the SPD, which demanded that the German princes who had lost power in 1918 should be expropriated without compensation. There was a good deal of sympathy for this plebiscite at the time, even among the middle classes whom the Great Inflation had left penniless. On the other hand, it represented a serious disregard of the principle of private property which was guaranteed by the Weimar Constitution. The north-west German NSDAP supported this plebiscite. It provided Hitler who sharply rejected the move with an opportunity to end his waiting game and assert his leadership over the Strasser wing. What he had found most irritating was a draft for a new and more 'socialist' programme which the *Arbeitsgemeinschaft* had worked out. For 14 February 1926 Hitler called a meeting of Nazi leaders at Bamberg. This meeting became an even more extreme repeat performance of the founding meeting at Munich a year earlier. Hitler spoke for hours developing his ideological and political views; he derided the left-wing proclivities of the north-westerners and their programmatic discussions as intellectual pie in the sky (*Spielerei*). He emphasised that it was vital to adhere unwaveringly to the old Twenty-Five Point Programme of 1920 as the symbol of the movement's unity. At the end of this monologue there was hardly opposition. Gregor Strasser raised a few feeble and unconvincing objections. Goebbels remained silent. Not too long ago, he had made the provocative remark that the 'little bourgeois Hitler' might have to be excluded from the party. Now, as his diary testifies, he was both infuriated by the 'awfully' reactionary views of Hitler and fascinated by the latter's drive and powers of expression which were far superior to those of all the other leaders.[9]

This was not the end to the infighting over the NSDAP's programme. Rather there occurred a 're-formation of fronts.'[10] However, Hitler had strengthened his leadership position. The aura of his superior leadership capacities now increasingly became an important factor which exerted a special attraction in favour of the Nazi movement among the other rival *völkische* parties and associations. What is no less significant is that Hitler did not demonstrate his leadership regularly through control of the party machine. Rather and as was his practice later as Reich Chancellor and head of state, he merely asserted it from time to time. It was as if he was 'floating' above the party. If up to 1928 the NSDAP succeeded in absorbing many activists of the former *Deutsch-Völkische Freiheitspartei*, of the Ludendorff movement and from the remnants of the radical paramilitary organisations, it was not because it had a better and more convincing programme. Rather it was primarily the more dynamic and charismatic figure of Adolf Hitler. In this connection it was an essential element that from 1927 onwards Hitler was again able to appear and speak in public.

The rivalry between Hitler and Gregor Strasser reflected divergent forces and aspects of the Nazi movement: on the one hand, the powerful suggestiveness and the aura of a charismatic missionary, on the other, the circumspect and loyal organising zeal of a selfless round-the-clock activist. This division of labour ultimately strengthened the attractiveness of the party as long as it did not affect the unity of the movement.

However, while the Weimar Republic experienced a phase of relative stability these intra-party developments made little impact on national politics. From 1926, the NSDAP participated in a number of regional elections but its showing was invariably depressingly poor. In the Saxon elections at the end of October 1926 it received a mere 1.6 per cent of the votes. The results of the Thuringian election at the beginning of the following year

9. See H. Heiber (ed.), *Das Tagebuch von Joseph Goebbels 1925/26*, Stuttgart 1961.
10. R. Kühnl, *Die nationalsozialistische Linke*, Meisenheim 1966, p. 43.

were somewhat better at 3.4 per cent. In Hamburg the share was once more 1.5 per cent in October 1927. A month later the figure in the Brunswick vote was 3.7 per cent. The national elections of 20 May 1928 confirmed that the party still had not come out of the political through three and a half years after Hitler had refounded it. Some 800,000 adult Germans (2.6 per cent of the total) cast their vote for the Nazis. Considering that the membership had reached almost the 100,000 mark, this was no doubt an extreme ratio between members and voters. It showed that the NSDAP was, at least for the moment, confined to a small, but activist hard core of fanatical supporters.

The election results also dissapointed the expectations of the left wing within the party. It had been in the provinces and small towns rather than in the working-class conurbations that the Nazi vote had risen above the average. This was particularly true of those regions in which a traditionally established Protestant and 'nationally-minded' middle class had come into sharp conflict politically and socially with equally strong battalions of the Social Democrat or Communist working class. It was in these areas that the radically anti-Marxist slogans of the NSDAP fell on particularly fertile soil. Bourgeois animosities and fears of being swamped by objectionable cultural and social forces were widespread in these circles. A number of towns in Franconia and Thuringia demonstrate this point, with Coburg being a particularly good example. Here the Nazis had been able to launch a violent 'penal expedition' against the 'Reds' as early as the autumn of 1922. They received the applause of the local bourgeoisie which was motivated by the above-mentioned fears and resentments. Having joined forces with a number of local middle-class parties, the NSDAP later managed to gain a bare absolute majority. This was on 23 June 1929, four months prior to 'Black Friday' on Wall Street which ushered in the Great Slump. Coburg thus became the first German town where the Nazis gained a dominant influence on the local council. It anticipated a development which was soon to occur also at regional level in the states of Brunswick and Thuringia.

While there was nothing inevitable about this incipient broadening of the Nazi's political base, the party had prepared this development in the years prior to 1928. By that time there were no sizeable alternative organisations left that might have provided a focus for a right-wing radical mass movement. Firmly moved forward by the strange certainty of its *Führer* Adolf Hitler that the decisive breakthrough was near, the NSDAP had meanwhile completed its organisational battle preparations, as if it had had prior information about the impending crisis. Many local bases had been created. In parallel to them the SA had been consolidated and been turned into a paramilitary arm which could be quickly expanded. These units were capable not only of engaging in aggressive verbal propaganda, but also of bringing to bear their real and visible combat strength. Finally there existed special professional associations such as the League of Nazi Lawyers (*NS-Rechtswahrerbund*) League of Nazi Doctors (*NS-Ärztebund*) and the League of Nazi Teachers (*NS-Lehrerbund*), which had been created before 1928. In that year then the NSBO, a Nazi trade union, was founded. All these organisations were held in readiness to penetrate a variety of spheres of interest articulation in German society. This strategy was comparable to that of the prewar Social Democratic Party whose sub-organisations likewise covered all areas of life. But in copying this example the NSDAP was at the same time on the way towards becoming what Siegmund Neumann has called an 'absolutist integration party' before developing, from 1929–30 onwards, into a mass movement.

Hitler, who displayed a most original creativity in this field, had grasped long ago that the promise of future successes which he held out in his many speeches was an indispensable stimulus for the party's activism. But he also realised that it would continue to be effective only if it did not remain merely a matter of consciousness, but could also express itself in visible symbols. The Reich Party Rally in August 1927, which was organised under Hitler's overlordship and at which his charisma was openly put into the limelight, is a good case in point. For the first time both the NSDAP and the SA had more or less achieved organisational cohesion and a uniform dress in 1927. SA and party formations, complete with banners, flags and marching bands, arrived in special trains from all over the country to appear before the romantic backdrop of the old city of Nuremberg. The Hitler Youth, which had been founded in the previous year, made its first appearance. Even Hitler donned a brownshirt which the SA had just introduced. The main rally in

Luitpoldshein culminated in the ceremonial consecration of twelve SA banners. After this Hitler, standing upright in an open convertible and holding up his arm, motionless, reviewed the march-past of his followers.

In other words, the party, which at this time got barely more than 2 or 3 per cent of the national vote, knew how to present itself at certain points in massive numbers. This caused the movement to look bigger to the outside world than it actually was. Moreover it provided the members with an emotional experience and strengthened their thirst for future action. Both factors were important preconditions of the party's subsequent success once the crisis had struck. They facilitated the crystallisation of the hopes, expectations and resentments of many frightened and disorientated men and women around this extremist movement.

2.3. *The Nazi Party as a Mass Movement in the Political and Economic Crisis of 1929–1933*

Hitler's unshakeable conviction that his movement would ultimately succeed was not merely based on his subjective feeling and the auto-suggestive dogmatism of his thoughts and aspirations. There were also objective reasons for his optimism. The period of relative prosperity and stabilisation from 1924 to 1928 had, it is true, resulted in a weakening of the right-wing radical potential and a certain moderation of the conservative Right embodied by the DNVP, the *Stahlhelm* ex-Servicemen's Association and the United Patriotic Leagues (VVVD). However, parliamentary democracy had not yet struck firmer roots. In fact there were many indications of a revival of time-honoured nationalist-conservative and even monarchist ideas, in particular among the upper classes and the bourgeoisie which saw themselves as the pillars of the state.

One symptomatic reflection of these backward-looking tendencies was the popular vote which, in April 1925, elevated the former Imperial Field Marshal von Hindenburg to the Reich presidency, following Ebert's death. To be sure, he obtained only a small relative majority on the second ballot, defeating the Catholic Centre Party leader, Wilhelm Marx, who had the support of the SPD, the non-Bavarian Catholics and the Democrats. Hindenburg's victory was indirectly due to the Communists who refused to withdraw their candidate, Ernst Thälmann, although he had no chance of winning; it was also due to the Bavarian Catholics (BVP) who were so opposed to appearing in a common front with the Social Democrats that they preferred to vote for a Protestant Prussian field marshal.

Nevertheless, the election of Hindenburg was nothing for a parliamentary republic to be proud about. The new president was an arch-conservative; a war hero who deep down in his heart had remained a monarchist and who felt no ties with liberal parliamentarism. Those 14 million Germans who had voted for him had done so not because they saw in him a representative of the Republic, but rather because to them he was a monument of past glorious battles. He was a sort of Ersatz-Kaiser representing the lost monarchy. At most he could serve as a symbol of the gradual reconciliation of the conservative Right with the Republic, provided of course he actually lived up to his reputation of staunch honesty and loyalty to the constitution which the republican papers respectfully credited him with. Stresemann, the leader of the German People's Party (DVP), also held these hopes despite the burden which the election of Hindenburg imposed upon his simultaneous policy of rapprochement with the Western powers. And they were not totally unjustified. In fact they were apparently confirmed in October 1926, following renewed conflict between Otto Gessler, the *Reichswehr* Minister and a member of the Democrats, and General von Seeckt, the military chief of the army. Seeckt had in a demonstrative manner allowed one of the Kaiser's sons to attend recent *Reichswehr* manoeuvres. Gessler wanted Seeckt dismissed, and he obtained Hindenburg's support for his decision. The move represented at the same time the long-delayed triumph of the civilian authorities over the vaingloriousness of the *Reichswehr*'s military leadership. On the other hand, the indications are that Hindenburg was moved more by his personal dislike of the arrogant Seeckt than by a belief in constitutional principles. This emerged at the latest at the beginning of 1928 when Gessler's successor was to be appointed. Hindenburg nominated the new *Reichswehr* Minister without consulting the Reich Chancellor, demonstrating that in this case he pro-

posed to use his constitutional right of nomination not merely
pro forma but also in substance. This violation of the spirit of the
Constitution was mitigated by the fact that General Groener,
who became Gessler's successor, was a 'republican by reason'.
On the other hand, the underlying structural problem remained
covered up, which was that the ex-field marshal and President
claimed to have a special relationship with the *Reichswehr* Ministry, reinforcing the process of presidential decision-making. The
end result of this development was that the *Reichswehr* leadership came to act in an advisorial capacity to the President and
ultimately even gained a decisive influence on the nomination of
the Reich Chancellor by the President. This explains why Kurt
von Schleicher, the head of the *Reichswehr* Ministry's central
office, was able to rise from 1928–9 to the position of the 'field-
grey eminence' of Weimar politics.

The President's ambiguity towards the Republic may be
gauged also by looking at other decisions. Thus, in May 1926, he
issued a decree concerning the national colours. It stipulated
that German diplomatic agencies overseas must display, side-
by-side with the Republic's black-red-golden colours, the black-
white-red of the Imperial flag which had continued to be the
colours of the merchant navy. A heated debate ensued which
led to the downfall of Reich Chancellor Hans Luther. But the
crucial point is that Hindenburg and his advisers had unnecess-
arily provoked this conflict. It was also worrying that the President accepted honorary membership in the right-wing *Stahlhelm*
ex-Servicemen's Association. This put him into the position of
protector of the association even after influential leaders abandoned their erstwhile relative moderation and from 1928 onwards proclaimed their fundamental and most vigorous opposition to the Weimar 'system'. An example of this radical anti-
republicanism was a resolution of the Brandenburg branch of
the *Stahlhelm* of September 1928 which contained the following
sentence: 'We hate the present constitutional structure with all
our heart because it blocks the prospect of liberating our enslaved fatherland.'[11]

However, it was also the fault of the parties and their parliamentary groups, if parliamentary democracy became increas-

11. Quoted in E. Eyck, *Geschichte der Weimarer Republik*, Erlenbach–Zürich 1956, vol. 2,
p. 217.

ingly discredited in these years and the President's influence was in the ascendancy. All too marked was their propensity to subordinate their responsibility for the stability of the republican political system as a whole to the interests of their party. The structural weaknesses of parliamentarism in the Weimar period were rooted in the Imperial period and were marked by a number of peculiarities. Thus Cabinet Ministers frequently found themselves deserted by their own parliamentary party. This in turn led to a destruction of the government coalition of the day and to frequent changes of government. Votes of no-confidence were often purely negative, resulting from the sum total of oppositional votes which came from very divergent political parties and were cast for widely differing motives. Finally coalition cabinets and parties did not feel a strong pressure to forge compromises and establish a consensus among themselves.

It was another characteristic of the restorative tendency which began to spread from 1924 onwards (and hence long before the crisis period of the late 1920s and early 1930s) that the Social Democrats were excluded from government participation. In the spring of 1927 a coalition of the non-socialist parties was formed which even included a number of ministers who belonged to the DNVP and who were by no means loyal to the existing republican system. One of them, the new Reich Minister of the Interior Walter von Keudell had occupied the position of *Landrat* (regional administrator) in the early postwar period and had been dismissed in 1920 because of his involvement in the Kapp Putsch. As Erich Eyck wrote, nominating him as guardian of the Constitution was like putting 'the goat in charge of the vegetable garden'.[12] One of his first official decisions was to relieve a number of first-class republican civil servants in his Ministry from their duties. Among them was Arnold Brecht, a highly qualified *Ministerialdirektor*, who looked after questions of constitutional reform. Brecht was subsequently taken into Otto Braun's Prussian government.

By 1928 the aversion of the middle-class parties to co-operate with the Social Democrats had become so strong that an impasse developed after the national elections in May of that year. The

12. Ibid. p. 142.

results of these elections made it practically impossible to form a new government without the Social Democrats, after the SPD had made considerable gains whereas the DNVP suffered serious losses. If it proved nevertheless possible to construct a left-centre coalition under a Social Democratic Reich Chancellor (Hermann Müller), the credit must go above all to Stresemann who had by then emerged as the most powerful political figure in republican politics. Yet even at the time of its formation, this 'Grand Coalition' practically overtaxed the capacity of the parties involved in it to keep within the ranks. Nor did Hindenburg conceal his own aversion to the Müller Cabinet. It collapsed at the end of March 1930, less than six months after Stresemann, the key figure holding the government together, had died and less than five months after Black Friday on the New York stock-market which ushered in the Great Depression. After these setbacks it did not take long for the latent tensions within the 'Grand Coalition' to rise to the surface.

The shock of the Great Inflation of 1923 had barely been overcome when the Great Slump shook the country's social and economic foundations. This nexus represents one of the major reasons of why Germany experienced a much greater degree of political radicalisation than other nations which were likewise hit by the Great Depression. However, this in itself does not explain why the pendulum swung towards the extreme Right in Germany and, contrary to the American or French experience, much less towards the Left. At the root of this particular development lay the crisis of legitimation which haunted the Weimar Republic since 1919 and in which nationalist issues continued to dominate. This crisis was determined much more decisively by the 'disloyal opposition' of the right-wing forces than by the anti-republicanism of the Communists.

This meant that the renewed social upheaval was moulded by the political developments which preceded it and in which the right-wing opposition played a major role from 1928 onwards. At first this movement was carried forward by the traditional agrarian elites of Prussia who had begun to suffer from a world-wide slump in demand for agricultural produce. In other words, agriculture went into economic decline even before industry and commerce were pushed into a reduction of their workforce. A brief review of the development of the agrarian sector is therefore called for.

Owing to the world war and the postwar economic controls, German agriculture had been virtually protected against foreign competition for a full decade between 1914 and 1924. Thereafter adjustment to world-market conditions and also to changing consumption habits suddenly became unavoidable. Agriculture had to move into high-class produce and to rationalise — a policy which was promoted by the banks, but which led to increased indebtedness from 1925–6 onwards. Agriculture was also faced with higher taxes which had resulted from the 1921 Finance Reform, but whose impact came to be felt only after the end of the Great Inflation from about 1925–6 onwards. By 1928 bankruptcies and cash flow problems which also affected the landed nobility and the provincial retailers had begun to assume crisis proportions in the agricultural regions of Germany. Thus between 1925 and 1927 the number of bankrupt farmsteads sold by auction averaged 31; by 1928 this figure had risen to 64, rocketing to 85 in 1929, 94 in 1930, 135 in 1931 and 190 in 1932.[13] These developments unleashed a massive protest movement which radically changed political conditions in the countryside from 1928 onwards. Schleswig-Holstein had once been an agricultural region with a strong liberal-democratic tradition. But as early as 1928 tens of thousands of farmers and peasants joined political demonstrations of a size which had hitherto been witnessed only among striking industrial workers. They became the precursors of the radical *Landvolk* movement which began in 1929 and which ultimately did not even shrink from violent means. There were a number of sensational bomb attacks on Inland Revenue premises which Hans Fallada wrote about in his fictional account of 1931, entitled *Bauern, Bonzen, Bomben*. It was a book which captured realities in the German countryside authentically as well as impressively.

The radical activism of the *Landvolk* soon spread to Oldenburg, Lower Saxony, Pomerania, East Prussia, Silesia and other agrarian provinces. This was the soil for the massive agitation of the Nazi Party which began in 1929–30. In fact, the Nazi campaign in provincial Germany could never have succeeded without it. It was also the time when there emerged in the rural

13. For details see R. Heberle, *Landbevölkerung und Nationalsozialismus*, Stuttgart 1963, pp. 97ff.

NSDAP a type of populist agitator who had his fingers on the pulse of the ordinary voter and who cunningly knew how to articulate and reinforce the worries and the sense of crisis felt by his audience. Hinrich Lohse, the *Gauleiter* for Schleswig-Holstein, or Carl Röver, the *Gauleiter* for Oldenburg, were early examplars of this new type. From the summer of 1930 onwards the NSDAP quickly became the leading agrarian movement. Soon it had won many local peasant leaders over to its side and had begun to penetrate agricultural associations and lobbies. It was helped in this by a centrally led propaganda apparatus which the Munich Headquarters had built up under Richard Walther Darré.

A comparison of the Nazis' performance in the 1928 national elections with the figures for 1930 tells this story of dramatic change. Thus the Nazi share in the rural constituencies of Schleswig-Holstein rose from 5.4 per cent to 35.1 per cent, mainly at the expense of the DNVP. The Nazis even scored averages of 40 per cent in rural communities with under 2,000 inhabitants in the western marshes and in the poor-soil regions further east. Oldenburg presented a similar picture. In 1930 the NSDAP achieved 27.3 per cent of the total vote and became the strongest party. In the predominantly Protestant rural districts it averaged 42.8 per cent and in some areas even over 50 per cent.[14]

A further consequence of the protest movement which proliferated in the North and East German countryside from 1928 onwards was that it shook other parties, political organisations and leagues such as the *Stahlhelm* out of their lethargic conservatism. Hitherto these associations had been dominated by rural notables and had shown a relative moderation. But now they began to voice their old reservations against the Weimar 'system' much more stridently, not least in order to ward off the populist offensive launched upon their members by the *Landvolk* and the NSDAP. These changes in the political atmosphere at the grass-roots quickly also made themselves felt at the level of the national executives of these organisations. As far as the DNVP was concerned, it was symptomatic of the changing political climate that Alfred Hugenberg, the 'press tsar', was

14. See K. Schaap, *Die Endphase der Weimarer Republik im Freistaat Oldenburg, 1928–1932*, Düsseldorf 1978, pp. 117f.

elected chairman.[15] Well-known as a *völkisch*-Pan-German nationalist since before the First World War, he replaced Kuno Count Westarp, an old Prussian conservative. A major cause of this change of leadership was a conflict within the DNVP centring on Walther Lambach, its representative on the executive of the large *Deutsch-nationaler Handlungsgehilfenverband* (Association of Lower-Ranking White-Collar Employees and Commercial Assistants). On the other hand, the election of Hugenberg who had close ties with heavy industry and had the reputation of an 'arch-reactionary' meant that the white-collar workers who had formed a major constituency of the DNVP became politically alienated. Subsequently more and more of these voters were absorbed by the NSDAP. Even Wilhelm Marx, the moderate leader of the Centre Party, called the election of Hugenberg, who was Stresemann's most vigorous opponent, 'a threat to the inner peace of Germany'.[16]

Yet another development, which also occurred before the onset of the Great Depression, was even more revealing of the change in the general political climate: on 9 July 1928 Hugenberg, the *Stahlhelm* leader Franz Seldte and Heinrich Class, the leader of the Pan German League and a close friend of Hugenberg's, formed a so-called 'Reich Committee'. This body was to coordinate a nation-wide campaign against the Young Plan reparations proposal and was to include Hitler. The basic outlines of the Young Plan had been worked out by an international commission of experts meeting in Paris in the spring of 1929. The proposals amounted to a considerable easing of German reparations obligations as laid down in the 1924 Dawes Plan. German payments which recently had been as high as 2.5 milliard [17] marks were to be reduced by 25 per cent. Above all, the Allies were to withdraw their reparations agent through whom they had exerted an international control over German finances. Moreover, the Allied policy of retaining German territories as pawns was to be abandoned and this implied the withdrawal of troops from the occupied parts of the Rhineland ahead of the schedule envisaged by the Versailles Treaty. On

15. See H. Holzbach, *Das 'System Hugenberg'. Die Organisation bürgerlicher Sammlungspolitik vor dem Aufstieg der NSDAP*, Stuttgart 1981, pp. 192ff.

16. Quoted in E. Eyck, op.cit., p. 216.

17. See F. Dickmann, 'Die Regierungsbildung in Thüringen als Modell der Machtergreifung', in *Vierteljahrshefte für Zeitgeschichte*, 14/1966, 462ff., also for the following.

the other hand, the burden placed upon the German economy by reparations payments still appeared horrifically high and long-term. The Allied experts thought that it would take another sixty years for the German debts to be cleared and for the funds owed by Britain and France to the United States to be repaid. The viability of the Young Plan, which was the subject of further negotiations at The Hague in the autumn and winter of 1929, depended first and foremost on the subsequent development of the German national economy. But this economy was now experiencing a sharp downturn and the deficit in the Reich budget grew dangerously. Inevitably the Young Plan discussions became tied up with a reform of the German system of finance and taxation and the earlier practice of placing, often all too recklessly, Reich loans in the domestic and foreign capital markets. The President of the *Reichsbank*, Hjalmar Schacht, who had himself acted for months as the top adviser of the Reich government at the Young Plan negotiations and who had himself supported the basic principles of that Plan, used this as a pretext to publish a sensational memorandum in which he brusquely dissociated himself from the government's policy and from the revised reparations agreement. When the Young Plan was finally ratified in March 1930, Schacht tendered his resignation. Subsequently, he became an exponent of the 'National Opposition', and from 1931-2 onwards he was probably the most influential among Hitler's advisers on matters of economic and fiscal policy.

To be sure, these developments could not be predicted when the anti-Young Plan 'Reich Committee' was formed in the summer of 1929. Its leaders initiated a plebiscite designed to reject the Plan. The defeat of this plebiscite was self-inflicted because, at Hitler's insistence, they combined their bill 'against the enslavement of the German people' with a threat to initiate criminal proceedings on grounds of treason against all German decision-makers supporting the Young Plan. As a result the campaign overshot its target and forced the more moderate critics of the Plan into the arms of the government. Ultimately the plebiscite which was held on 22 December 1929 attracted no more than 12 per cent of the voters.

Hitler linked up with the 'Reich Committee' although he expected the campaign to fail and despite the aversion of the left wing in his party against 'reactionaries' like Hugenberg. He apparently did so in the expectation that a joint campaign would present the NSDAP with an excellent opportunity to move in the political limelight at a time when the party still operated on the margins of the right-wing opposition movement. No doubt this was an accurate calculation. For one, the joint campaign turned the NSDAP into an acceptable ally within the camp of the 'National Opposition'. Moreover, it gained the support of the powerful Hugenberg press empire at no cost to itself. At the same time it did not find it difficult to outdo its allies in the DNVP and the *Stahlhelm* by its well-worn methods of an extremely aggressive propaganda. Thus it was able to seize the opportunity of advertising itself as the most radical protest movement in the country during a period when the Great Depression made its first impact on German society.

The political consequences of a 'Reich Committee' campaign soon emerged in Thuringia. Since the autumn of 1923, when the Reich government sent in the army to remove the existing left-wing coalition, Thuringia had been controlled by an "anti-Marxist Block of Order", composed of *Landbund*, DVP, DNVP, DDP and *Wirtschaftspartei* which held a slim majority *vis-à-vis* the working-class parties. Since 1927 the NSDAP held two seats in the Thuringian Diet and hence had been without significance in the politics of the province. This picture changed dramatically when the propaganda against the Young Plan set in. The *Landbund* and the *Wirtschaftspartei* (as a representation of the more well-to-do middle classes) were strong in this region and they now joined in. This enabled the NSDAP to proclaim a joint front, thereby splitting the Thuringian government in which both DVP and DDP were also represented right down the middle. Fresh elections were called for 8 December 1929. The NSDAP obtained 11.3 per cent, mainly at the expense of DVP, DNVP and *Landbund*. The Party had trebled its 1928 share and for the first time burst through the 10 per cent mark at *Land* level. In the small towns and villages of the Thuringian Forest, where the economic crisis had early on taken a heavy toll among the small producers of toys and Christmas decorations, the Nazis were even able to increase their share fivefold.[18]

The Thuringian result was particularly explosive because the NSDAP with its six out of fifty-three seats had come to occupy the position of balancer between the socialist parties (with their 24 seats) and the 'bourgeois' parties (with their 23 seats). The 'anti-Marxist' government could not continue without Nazi support. In these circumstances Hitler decided ruthlessly to exploit the situation. He personally intervened in the negotiations with the middle-class parties and demanded that the NSDAP be given the important Ministries of the Interior and of Education. His ministerial candidate was his old Bavarian supporter Dr Wilhelm Frick who, like Hitler, had been sentenced in 1924 for his role in the Beerhall Putsch of November 1923. More recently he had been made leader of the Nazi Reichstag faction, a position in which he had excelled by his reckless attacks against Stresemann's DVP. When the negotiations threatened to founder because of Frick and his record, Hitler personally travelled to Weimar on 10 January 1930. He issued a three-day ultimatum to the leaders of the middle-class parties. He then made a speech before an assembly of Thuringian industrialists reassuring them that the aims of the Nazis were constitutional and favoured industry and commerce. But most astonishing of all, he succeeded all round. Only the left–liberal DDP could not be won over to an alliance with the Nazis. The national–liberal DVP, on the other hand, overcame its scruples and gave in to Hitler's demands. The shift towards the Right set in earlier at the provincial level than in the party's national executive which was now bereft of Stresemann. As Hitler explained three weeks later, a decisive factor which tipped the scales in Frick's favour was 'a very strong pressure' which important industrial circles exerted in Weimar upon the DVP.[19]

This admission is contained in a long personal letter which Hitler sent to a foreign admirer of the NSDAP on 3 February 1930. The letter also contained a very clear exposition of the aims which the Nazis hoped to achieve in the Thuringian government and which had been agreed with Frick. All in all, the document provides a deep insight into how Hitler saw the situation of his party at this juncture when it was about to become a mass movement. He was also particularly frank about

18. See H. Braun, 'Das Ministerium Frick in Thüringen (1930/32) als Beispiel national-sozialistischer Regierungspolitik vor 1933', unpubl. MA dissertation, University of Munich, 1972, p. 10f.

19. European usage = 1,000 million.

why he had been so keen to gain control of the Ministries of the Interior and of Education. The former, he argued, was in charge not only of the police, but also of the entire Thuringian civil service, with powers to nominate and dismiss administrators. The Education Ministry supervised the entire school and university system as well as the state theatres: 'Whoever occupies these two ministries and ruthlessly and patiently exploits the power that comes with them can achieve extraordinary things'. Of course, what the Nazis required was a person who was not only a fanatical adherent of the party, but also an experienced civil servant. Frick, he concluded, possessed these qualities. Hitler then talked about the gradual purges which Frick would launch in the Thuringian civil service and above all among the police forces. Secondly, the school system was to be put into the service of turning every German 'into a fanatical nationalist'. Left-wing and republican teachers were to be removed and curricula to be adapted to Nazi ideas. At the University of Jena a chair for race questions was to be established. Thuringia, which, he argued, had been 'the starting point of several great intellectual renovations', would thus once more provide the base of another reformation. Finally Hitler mentioned, not without considerable pride, how the work of the previous years was beginning to bear fruit and how luck was on the side of the untiring organiser and skillful propagandist.

There can be little doubt that the Thuringian case represented a model for the Nazi seizure of power in 1933. But Frick's energetic attempts to change the education system and especially to introduce Nazi ideology and racist teaching had rather a negative reception among the German public. His moves to Nazify the Thuringian police and civil service met with effective opposition, in particular on the part of the Reich Minister of the Interior. A little over a year later, Nazi forays into Thuringian politics had so alienated the DVP in the government that it joined forces with the Social Democrats and on 1 April 1931 passed a motion of no-confidence in Frick. The Nazi minister had to go. It took the Nazis until the end of September 1932 to rejoin the government. By this time they were led by *Gauleiter* Fritz Sauckel and had gained 42 per cent of the vote. Antisocialist coalitions along the Thuringian pattern of 1930 came about in Brunswick on 1 October 1930 and in Mecklenburg-

Strelitz on 6 April 1932. And thanks to the major electoral successes of 1932 the Nazis even succeeded in putting themselves at the head of the governments of the small provinces of Sachsen-Anhalt (21 May 1932), Oldenburg (16 June 1932) and Mecklenburg-Schwerin (13 July 1932). Initially promising moves to join government coalitions, on the other hand, came to nought in the more important *Länder* of Saxony in October 1930 and Hesse in November/December 1931. There was also the toleration of minority cabinets in Prussia and a number of South German states which was agreed among the anti-Nazi groupings in order to prevent a governmental takeover by the NSDAP.

The Nazi balance-sheet of its attempts to assume government responsibility is hence not particularly impressive. On the other hand, they contributed to the appearance that the Hitler movement was capable of working in cabinet positions. The main reason for the failure was the party's own primarily negative strategy of obstruction and agitation. It was a strategy which Hitler and Goebbels (who had been put in charge of overall propaganda in the Reich in 1930) time and again reverted to — a strategy which did not try to overcome the government crises resulting from the Slump, but rather aimed recklessly to exploit and reinforce these crises. Opposition to this negative approach arose even inside the NSDAP. Brunswick represents a particularly glaring case in point. In July 1931 Anton Franzen, the Nazi Minister of the Interior and of Education, resigned in protest against Hitler's obstructionism. After violent clashes with Hitler, Franzen subsequently left the party.

Nevertheless, the NSDAP was tremendously successful from the autumn of 1929 onwards as a movement which rallied nationalist and social protest voters opposed to existing conditions. In this respect the party benefited from the economic crisis, but also, just as in 1923, from the basic affinity towards it among the conservative upper classes in the army and civil service, in the lobbies of the agrarians, the bourgeoisie and industry. Their strong anti-republicanism led them to see themselves as potential allies of the Nazis.

The DVP, which was close to big business, similarly turned towards the anti-republican Right. This reorientation was not merely a consequence of Stresemann's death who had played an indispensable role of integration at the parliamentary level; it was also a reflection of the slump in production and demand affecting industry and the growing criticism of the Weimar welfare system. This criticism was by now almost identical to the rejection of parliamentarism which, the employers argued, gave the unionised workforce an excessively large influence on the social, financial and economic policies of the Reich. Similar arguments could be heard among the agrarians, whose 'Green Front' had been incited by the agricultural crisis to take a recklessly aggressive stance towards the republican parliamentary system. Its aggressiveness was dampened down merely in the Catholic parts of Germany where the Centre Party (or its Bavarian branch, the BVP) exerted a moderating influence and partially succeeded in retaining the loyalty of the rural population.

Meanwhile the Reich government of the 'Grand Coalition' soldiered on; it contained, apart from Chancellor Müller, three other Social Democrats: Rudolf Wissell (Labour), Rudolf Hilferding (Finance) and Carl Severing (Interior). From the autumn of 1929 these men became all the more the target of the radical opposition front against the Weimar 'system' because burning issues of the day like the recovery of public finances were intimately linked with the pressure to adapt welfare benefits payable by the government and the employers to the rapidly growing army of unemployed. In the late autumn of 1929 there occurred a sharp conflict between SPD and DVP in the Cabinet over the question of whether the employers' contribution to the unemployment benefit scheme should be raised from 3 per cent to 3.5 per cent of pay before tax and other deductions beyond 30 June 1930. It was over this question that the last government of the Republic with a parliamentary majority finally fell apart at the end of March 1930. Unlike Müller, the SPD Reichstag faction was no longer prepared to make further concessions and hence contributed its share to the collapse of the Cabinet. But this collapse was not inevitable. It could have been prevented or, at least, delayed, if Hindenburg had been prepared to empower a Social Democratic Reich Chancellor to settle the matter by means of a presidential emergency decree. This is what Ebert had granted to Stresemann in 1923–4, and Hindenburg allowed his 'own' chancellors, Brüning and

Papen, to resort to this solution from 1930 onwards. Müller was not so lucky.

In fact Müller's fall and the nomination of a new and more right-wing government had been prepared weeks in advance by Hindenburg's advisers. It was to be a government which would be less dependent on the Reichstag and more congenial to the President. And Heinrich Brüning had been earmarked to become Müller's successor long before the latter's resignation. Brüning, the leader of the parliamentary faction of the Centre Party, was a conscientious man on the right wing of the Catholics. Above all, he had more the making of an expert in matters of financial policy than of a thoroughbred in politics. Hindenburg was also preoccupied well before the end of March with the problem of how a new chancellor, to be nominated by him, might gain the support of the Right. The question uppermost in his mind was how Hugenberg's DNVP which had suffered a setback in the Young Plan plebiscite as well as the exit of its moderate wing might be persuaded to give its partial support to a new cabinet. Thus Hindenburg's State Secretary Otto Meissner explained to Count Westarp, the former leader of the DNVP Reichstag faction, as early as 15 January 1930 that 'a government crisis was expected by February or March triggered by the [problem of the] reform of public finances'. Hindenburg, Meissner continued, wanted to know from Westarp 'in strict confidence', if the President could count on 'direct or indirect support among the DNVP' for a new government he intended to constitute. Hindenburg was said by his State Secretary to be concerned 'that the opportunity of forming an anti-parliamentary and anti-Marxist' government (!) might again be lost. In that case the President would find it impossible ever to 'get away from governing with the Social Democrats'. Subsequently Westarp also learned from Hindenburg personally how worried he was about 'missing the boat again' and about 'being put in a tight spot in respect of having to carry on governing with the Social Democrats'.[20]

What therefore emerged in these preliminary discussions

20. Thus Count Westarp in the Note which he prepared on 15 January 1930 following his meeting with Hindenburg earlier that day, repr. in I. Maurer and U Wengst (eds.), *Politik und Wirtschaft in der Krise, 1930–1932, Quellen zur Ära Brüning*, part I, Düsseldorf 1980, pp. 15ff.

were the contours of the structural problem which a future Brüning Cabinet, which was half-dependent on the Reichstag and half-dependent on the President, would have to face. The idea was not to form a government whose members had been nominated by the parties, but one formed by a Chancellor who was a presidential nominee and relying on experts without party affiliations. On the other hand, such a cabinet still required 'toleration' by the Reichstag majority. Under the Constitution, parliament continued to have the right to rescind presidential emergency decrees through a majority vote. This peculiar situation gave rise to the temptation to govern, at least temporarily, without the Reichstag by sending it on leave or by dissolving it. To be sure, this was not a permanent solution as the Constitution required the holding of national elections sixty days after a dissolution of parliament at the latest. This was the dilemma in which Brüning quickly found himself in June–July 1930 after he had prepared a number of controversial emergency decrees aimed to put public finances on an even keel. He wanted to push through these decrees as soon as possible. He knew he had the full support of Hindenburg and therefore did not wish to be delayed by attempts to find a parliamentary majority prepared to tolerate these decrees. Hence his decision to dissolve the Reichstag on 18 July 1930. Fresh elections were necessary within three months and were, in fact, held on 14 September. In short, these elections which resulted in sensational gains for the Nazis were a consequence of the new system of semi-parliamentary, semi-presidential government instituted in March 1930.

During its eight-week election campaign the NSDAP succeeded in winning some 6.4 million voters, 18.3 per cent of the total. It thus became the second strongest party behind the SPD (24.5 per cent) and ahead of the Catholic Centre Party/BVP with their 14.8 per cent. How effectively the Nazi campaign had mobilised fresh support, emerges from a comparison with preceding regional elections. In the Thuringian elections ten months earlier where the turnout had been 75 per cent, the Nazis gained some 90,000 voters. By September 1930, when the turnout in Thuringia rose to 84 per cent, the Nazi total was 244,000. The gains in Saxony are even more striking. The elections for the Diet in June 1930 produced 375,000 votes for the NSDAP on an 73 per cent turnout, but three months later it received 561,000 votes on an 86 per cent turnout. The league table of Nazi successes was headed by the Protestant and agrarian regions of Schleswig-Holstein (27 per cent), Pomerania (24.3 per cent) and Hanover South-Brunswick (24.3 per cent). But significantly high percentages were also achieved in the mixed agricultural and small-scale industrial districts of Lower Silesia-Breslau (24.2 per cent), Chemnitz-Zwickau (23.8 per cent) and Rhineland-Palatinate (22.8 per cent). These areas even overtook the eastern agrarian constituencies of Posen-West Prussia (22.7 per cent) and East Prussia (22.5 per cent). Urban-industrial or Catholic districts came at the bottom of the scale: Berlin (12.8 per cent), Lower Bavaria (12.1 per cent), North Westphalia (12.0 per cent). A predominantly industrial structure and strong religious ties made two regions particularly resistant to Nazism: Upper Silesia (9.5 per cent) and Württemberg (9.4 per cent).

As the economic situation worsened and reached its peak in the following year, Nazi support continued to rise steeply. Thus local government elections were held at Bremen on 30 November 1930, ten weeks after the national elections in which the NSDAP had scored 25.6 per cent. Now the party doubled its share. In May 1931 it achieved 37 per cent in Oldenburg, thus becoming the largest party in this area. Its share in the Hesse Diet elections of November 1931 was likewise 37 per cent. However, this was almost the upper limit of what the Nazis were able to gain until 1933. Hitler attracted 36.8 per cent of the voters in the presidential elections of March–April 1932 in which he was a candidate. The Prussian elections of 12 April 1932 gave the NSDAP 38.3 per cent. A few months later, during the Reichstag elections of 31 July 1932, the percentage was 37.8.

Within two years the NSDAP had grown from a radical splinter party into a mass movement. It had changed the framework of politics in Germany in a revolutionary way and mopped up above all the former adherents of the 'bourgeois parties'. At the end of 1924 these parties (DNVP, DVP, DDP, *Wirtschaftspartei* and agrarian parties) had attracted some 47 per cent of the voting population. Four years later, their share was still 39 per cent. But in September 1930 the combined share slumped to 24 per cent and finally reached a low of 10 per cent in the national elections of 31 July 1932. Within this spectrum the shrinking of the liberal groups (DVP and DDP) was most marked. At the beginning of the Weimar Republic they had commanded the confidence of some 20 per cent of the voters. By 1928 this share had dropped back to 13.6 per cent, largely in favour of groupings specifically appealing to the economic interests of the middle classes and the farming community. In 1930 some 8.3 per cent cast their vote for the two parties. In the July elections of 1932 it was a mere 2.2 per cent. By this time the NSDAP had also absorbed most of the *Wirtschaftspartei* and the agrarian parties. In 1928 these groups had still gained the support of some 11 per cent of the voting population. By the summer of 1932, the *Wirtschaftspartei* achieved no more than 0.4 per cent, the agrarian groupings gained a miserable 0.2 per cent.

The losses of the DNVP were no less dramatic. At the end of 1924 it was the dominant conservative–nationalist movement polling 20 per cent. The agricultural crisis and the rise of the *Landvolk* had reduced it to 14 per cent by 1928. By 1930 its share was 7 per cent and a mere 5.9 per cent in the July elections of 1932. Again the Nazis were virtually the exclusive beneficiaries. In particular in the Protestant regions of the Reich where the DNVP had relied on the mass of peasants and members of the old and the new *Mittelstand*, these voters began to join the NSDAP. As a nationalist opposition party it was more radical, but also more populist and seemingly more concerned with the plight of these strata. As early as 1930 the Nazis won more than half of the traditional DNVP voters in the districts of Merseburg or Hesse-Nassau and in the city of Hamburg. The shift was even more striking in Schleswig-Holstein and in Lower Silesia. Here the DNVP lost 70 per cent of its former supporters and in Protestant Franconia the share was even 80 per cent in 1930, with the NSDAP being almost the sole beneficiary. The agrarian parts of East Elbia, the traditional stronghold of the DNVP, witnessed a desertion to the Nazis in two stages during 1930 and 1932. The table below demonstrates this shift for the provinces of East Prussia and Pomerania.

In both provinces the combined vote of the two working-class parties (SPD and KPD) remained the same between 1928 and 1932. They obtained some 350,000 votes in East Prussia and some 330,000 votes in Pomerania. The Catholic Centre Party was insignificant in Pomerania or retained its 80,000 East Prussian supporters. This is why it is easy to pinpoint the source of

May 1928	East Prussia	Pomerania
DNVP	312,000 (31.3%)	373,000 (41.6%)
NSDAP	16,000 (1.4%)	13,000 (1.5%)
September 1930		
DNVP	205,000 (19.6%)	242,000 (24.0%)
NSDAP	236,000 (22.5%)	237,0000 (24.3%)
July 1932		
DNVP	107,000 (9.5%)	168,000 (15.8%)
NSDAP	536,000 (47.1%)	511,000 (47.9%)

the two-stage gains for the Nazis in the two provinces: two fifths — some 200,000 of the 500,000 voters — were captured from the DNVP; the same number moved over from the other middle-class parties. One fifth finally came from previous non-voters.

The average for the whole of Germany also shows that the two working-class parties retained the loyalty of their 13.2 million voters. Similarly the forces of political Catholicism (Centre Party/BVP) remained stable at about 5.8 million. However, there was a marked shift amongst the working-class parties away from the Social Democrats towards the Communists. In May 1928 the respective shares were 9.1 million for the SPD and 3.2 million for the KPD; by July 1932 the figures were 7.9 million for the SPD and 5.3 million for the KPD.

The denominational divide in Germany was at least as important to the success or failure of the Nazis as social stratification. Hitler's party attracted large parts of the church-going population in the Protestant regions. This was particularly true of areas where the NSDAP masqueraded as an advocate of a 'positive Christianity' and as a patriotic movement of social and moral renewal. The Franconian Nazi leader Hans Schemm was particularly good at this. In these parts the NSDAP also received support from the 'German Christians' even before 1933. Nor was it unusual in Franconia, Thuringia or elsewhere for the local Protestant minister to don a brown shirt and to act as Nazi missionary in his parish. The Catholic Church, on the other hand, kept its distance from the NSDAP until 1933. In 1930–1 most bishops issued circulars to their flocks warning them that membership in the Nazi Party was incompatible with Catholicism. In 1930 this criticism received powerful confirmation when Alfred Rosenberg published his *Myth of the 20th Century*. In it Rosenberg was quite unambiguous not only about anti-Semitic, but also the anti-Catholic principles on which the *völkische* ideas of National Socialism were based. The book had a negative impact, and it appears that even Hitler felt embarrassed by its publication. Nor could the damage be made good by a demonstrative visit by Hermann Göring to Rome and by subsequent propaganda pamphlets trying to prove the compatibility of 'National Socialism and Catholic Church'.[21] Both the Catholic Church and the Centre Party (or its Bavarian branch, the BVP) remained fairly strong bulwarks against Nazism up to the beginning of 1933. A similar point applies to Social Democratic and Communist voters.

If a comparison is made between the national elections of May 1928 and of July 1932, both the two working-class parties and the two Catholic parties succeeded in attracting about a third of the six million erstwhile non-voters who had become politically mobilised by the Slump. But the main beneficiaries were the Nazis who owed about 30 per cent of their electoral victory of July 1932 to these new recruits. Among these the share of young voters who found the NSDAP most appealing was particularly high. What attracted them was the Nazi image as a party of youth. There was also the pressure of youth unemployment with its demoralising impact. In this way young people became politicised at an early age and in turn began markedly to shape the public style of the NSDAP and the SA. No less than 43 per cent of the 720,000 new members who entered the Nazi Party between 1930 and 1933 were under 30 years of age. With reference to the Oschatz-Grimma district in Saxony, it has been calculated that the cohorts of eighteen to thirty made up a mere 19 per cent in the local SPD; the equivalent figure for the NSDAP was 61 per cent. These high percentages are corroborated by many contemporary accounts. They confirm that it was in particular young people of traditional liberal–bourgeois or conservative family background who dissociated themselves from their parents' political outlook and joined the NSDAP.

21. Thus the title of a pamphlet by Johannes Stark, a Catholic university professor, published by the Nazi Eher-Verlag.

The main social basis of the Nazi mass movement was therefore the broad spectrum of the Protestant middle classes in town
and country. As early as 1930, the sociologist Theodor Geiger
explained the political landslide of the September elections in
terms of a 'panic among the *Mittelstand*'.[22] He argued that *fear* of
proletarianisation was an even stronger motive among large
parts of the old and the new *Mittelstand* than their *actual* degree
of material deprivation. Although objectively, these groups
were becoming proletarianised, their anti-proletarian and anti-
socialist consciousness which had been moulded by their education and social background held them back from voting for the
left-wing parties. Instead they began to search for a third way
between socialism and capitalism, and it was the Nazis who
promised it with their emotionally very effective propaganda
extolling the *Volksgemeinschaft*. Only a few people in the socialist
movement recognised at the time that the massive successes of
the NSDAP among peasant and the impoverished lower middle
classes were partly a consequence of a dogmatic Marxism; for all
this type of Marxism was able to offer the panic-stricken 'petty
bourgeoisie' and peasants was a 'proletarian class consciousness' against which they had developed a psychological block.

Up to 30 January 1933 the membership of the NSDAP rose to
about 800,000. Meanwhile the SA, in which Röhm had resumed
the leadership in January 1931 after Pfeffer's resignation, also
developed into a mass organisation of close to half a million
members. The SA's main task remained to provide protection to
the NSDAP during election campaigns which now never
seemed to end. At the same time, however, Röhm tried to
provide a military training, thereby reviving the early traditions
of paramilitarism. Soon after his nomination he also succeeded
in establishing contact with the *Reichswehr* Ministry and with
Schleicher in particular. The question was above all as to
whether SA men should participate in the voluntary border
protection units (*Grenzschutz*) in the East.

The membership statistics which were compiled in 1935[23]
clearly show that the self-employed ('old') *Mittelstand* and the
white-collar employee ('new') *Mittelstand* among the NSDAP
and SA were heavily overrepresented by comparison with blue-

22. T. Geiger, 'Panik im Mittelstand', in *Die Arbeit*, 1930, p. 654.
23. See *Partei-Statistik (Stand 1935)*, 3 vols., Munich n.d.

collar workers. On the other hand, the statistics listed some 28 per cent of the new members as 'workers'. It seems that the party and the SA had in this case succeeded in winning over parts of the unemployed, the majority of whom had moved to the KPD before 1933. But there were also land labourers, journeymen and skilled blue-collar workers from small, patricharchically organised enterprises and workshops. The Free Trade Unions had never really been able to gain a foothold among these workers. Finally there were blue-collar as well as white-collar workers who had previously been close to liberal, Christian-social or nationalist associations. Hitler refused permission for founding Nazi trade unions. Nevertheless, the NSBO became a party formation with certain trade union characteristics from 1931 onwards. It published a journal, *Arbeitertum*, and gained nearly 300,000 members up to the end of 1932. Berlin remained its centre where in 1932 Goebbels proclaimed a vigorous struggle against 'shop-floor Marxism'.[24] Under the slogan: 'No workshop without a Nazi cell' he started an extensive campaign of 'going into the factories'. However, Gregor Strasser became the most convincing promoter and exponent of the NSBO and of the 'national socialism' it represented. In a speech in the Reichstag on 10 May 1932 he powerfully appealed to the 'anti-capitalist longing' of the masses who had been hit and terrified by the Slump.

Compared with the strength of the Free Trade Unions, the NSBO was no more than a marginal phenomenon. Nevertheless, within the party itself, it became an organisation of considerable importance and engaged in special activities. It recognised the right to strike and organised the participation of Nazi workers in various local stoppages. The joint strike against with the Communists against the Berlin Transport Company from 3–8 November 1932 was the most sensational action the NSBO engaged in. It also represented a typical example of the highly diverse sub-organisations into which the NSDAP had divided up since becoming a mass movement. There were great contradictions between the agricultural programme which Darré had developed, the 'socialist' postulates of the NSBO and, thirdly, the demands of the 'NS Fighting Association of the

24. H.-G. Schumann, *Nationalsozialismus und Gewerkschaftsbewegung*, Hanover-Frankfurt 1958, pp. 38ff.

Commercial and Industrial *Mittelstand'* formed at the end of 1932. These contradictions provided critics of Nazism time and again with fresh ammunition in these years. On the other hand, its diversity helped the Hitler movement to gain the reputation of a 'people's party' which encompassed all strata of society. From 1930 onwards there was also a Nazi Women's League and an 'NS Fighting Association for German Culture'.

The need to integrate all these heterogeneous elements with their branches and subdivisions made it all the more vital for Hitler to act as the leader holding the movement together. The Nazi movement was far from coherent in ideological and organisational terms and this required a counterweight which Hitler's charismatic personality provided. There was an inner logic to the Hitler cult reaching new heights as the NSDAP developed into a mass movement. Since being a mass movement meant mass publicity, the aura surrounding, Hitler began to spread more widely both inside and outside the Nazi Party. This development became one of the crucial preconditions of his impact on the population. There are many reports in newspapers, police files and memoirs by participants relating to this impact during the election campaigns in 1930–2. They demonstrate to what extent the *Führer* was regarded with awe by the simple folk as a political 'shaman' (*'Wundermann'*). He was awaited and later showered with naïvely credulous applause. Nazi propaganda systematically inflated his legendary prestige, and there was the immediate impact of his rhetoric. Both aspects could ultimately no longer be separated and reinforced each other. There was the naïve popular faith in a political saviour which fed on the escalating crisis. There was also the organisation of innumerable mass rallies which were increasingly geared towards Hitler. They, too, reinforced each other and made Hitler more than ever before in the party's history indispensable for its popularity. The oppositional press frequently scrutinised 'Great Adolf' in critical or sarcastic terms.[25] But often it inadvertently contributed to augmenting his reputation. There were moreover many conservative, national–liberal or unpolitically provincial papers which paid voluntary tributes to Hitler's charisma even before 1932.

25. See I. Kershaw, *Der Hitler-Mythos*, Stuttgart 1980, pp. 34ff.

During the major election campaigns of 1932, Hitler was increasingly referred to in the Nazi press as our *Führer* or simply as the *Führer*. Day after day the impression was given of a movement which was united through its leader — a movement which gained its successes through him and found itself unstoppably and determinedly on the march towards assuming power in Germany. In 1932 Hitler used a plane on four campaign trips, ambiguously advertised in the Nazi press under the slogan of 'Hitler over Germany'. In the course of these trips he spoke to an average of 10,000 — 20,000 people at each of the 148 rallies he attended. For millions of Germans it became a kind of popular political sport during that year to have seen Hitler at least from a great distance and to have heard him speak at least through a loudspeaker.

Meanwhile the Nazi Party maintained its relentless radicalism and even increased it considerably. 'Bloody Sunday', staged in Hamburg-Altona on 17 July 1932, was merely a particularly extreme example of this radicalism. But these excesses barely diminished the effect of Hitler's charismatic hold over the masses. The physical struggle between Nazis and Communists had long become part of the political confrontation in the urban centres. The Nazis claimed to exert force in order to 'cleanse' Germany of Marxist and Jewish corruption of the nations, and in the climate of increased political agitation and social tension which obtained during the escalating economic and political crisis, such claims frequently met with 'understanding' on the part of the 'proper' bourgeoisie. At the same time the expansion of the NSDAP into a people's party also changed its public image. There were SA contingents in the cities whose main occupation was brawling; but there were others in the Protestant provinces that would jointly march to church on Sundays. In the cities SA men would engage in night-time muggings of Communists. But in day time these same contingents would capture the sympathies of the poor by organising soup-kitchens and collections for those in need. Its quantitative growth moreover changed the social composition of the Hitler movement. Local notables who in 1930 had not yet dared to show their sympathies for the NSDAP in public now began to abandon their reserve. It was no longer so easily possible or credible to dub the party as a bunch of radical putschists. After all, it now had the support of some 30 per cent of the population. Increasingly the 'old hardcore' of 'fanatical' ideologues and activists came to be surrounded by heterogeneous groupings of supporters who were more emotionally motivated and had moved over from the broad front of nationalist anti-republicanism. Hitler took account of these shifts in his 1932 campaign speeches. Less than before he would talk about the basic ideological principles of Nazism such as its radical anti-Semitism. Instead he would advance vague, but appealing slogans concerning the need to overcome party and class differences within the framework of a German *Volksgemeinschaft*.

Supporting the NSDAP did not necessarily mean at this juncture that one subscribed to a party with an extremist ideology. Many Germans, especially among the younger generation, were moved by hopes of greater social equality as well as mobility. They wanted a party which was close to the pulse of the people and they aspired to a social rejuvenation of the political institutions and interest groups. The pathos of renovation and youth which the party promoted no doubt also pinpointed various petrifications and immobilities which afflicted German society.

The notion of *Volksgemeinschaft* was next to the *Führer* cult one of the most effective slogans of Nazi propaganda. But it was not just harking back, in a reactionary fashion, to past feudal forms of organisation. It also represented an appeal to overcome the relicts of pre-bourgeois, pre-industrial social hierarchies and norms. It was a call to establish a more modern and more mobile bourgeois–nationalist mass society. These impulses for social innovation and modernisation were tied up in many contradictory ways with a resort to images of the past. But without reference to these former impulses it is difficult to explain the massive successes of the Nazi movement and its dynamic energies.

3
The Process of the Nazi Assumption of Power

The question of a Nazi participation in the Reich government was on the agenda of Weimar politics since the fateful elections of September 1930. And yet it took another two and a half years before Hitler was nominated Reich Chancellor, notwithstanding the fact that, judging by the results of several state elections, the NSDAP had, from 1931 onwards, become the largest political party in Germany. This time-lag alone shows that the assertion of the NSDAP's political power during the final years of the Weimar Republic proceeded far from smoothly. Nor was it relentless. However, the room for counteraction on the part of those forces which might have stopped Hitler kept on shrinking successively. Karl Dietrick Bracher has interpreted the transformation of the constitution and of constitutional reality in an authoritarian direction (which the presidential cabinets engaged in since March 1930) as part of the 'disintegration of republican power'. On the other hand, it should not be overlooked that the new constitutional reality also contained opportunities for a stabilisation of republican state power against right-wing and left-wing extremism, especially in the first year of the Brüning Cabinet. It was only in the final phase and in particular during the Papen era between June and November 1932 that the presidential system was tilted towards the extreme Right and began to move on a slippery slope. This was the phase when advance concessions were made which created the conditions of an assumption of power by the Nazis.

Nevertheless, it was no coincidence that the crisis of parliamentary democracy took a different path in Germany if compared with a number of East Central European countries, like Poland, Austria, Yugoslavia and Rumania. Owing to the socioeconomic crises and domestic political tensions, the parliamentary systems of these states also collapsed in the 1920s and

93

1930s. They were replaced by authoritarian governments or monarchical and military dictatorships. On the whole these systems proved capable of blocking the power ambitions of emerging fascist movements in their countries. This is why they have been judged rather more generously by historians and have been classified as 'educational dictatorships'[1] designed to put these societies back on an even keel. The presidential cabinets at the end of the Weimar Republic did not succeed in a stabilisation of this type which bridged and ultimately overcame the crisis. Nor was it just the intrigues of individuals and certain interest groups which led to the downfall of Brüning and Schleicher and finally of the Republic as a whole. Rather it was also the different constitutional framework and stage of socioeconomic development which German society had reached in comparison with the agricultural countries of East Central Europe. German society had become more highly politicised; the population was more involved in the debate on national, social and ideological questions, not least after the profoundly unsettling experiences of total war, revolution and economic crisis since 1914. In these circumstances a return to an authoritarian state paternalism had much less of a chance in Germany than in the less 'developed' societies further east. After the disappointments of parliamentary democracy, many Germans saw National Socialism as a persuasive alternative. It seemed to offer a strong determined leadership, a pseudo-democratic mobilisation of the masses and their participation in the promised national revival; it looked like a 'third way' between democracy and the state authoritarianism of the olden days. Herein lay the lure of Nazism.

3.1. *The Brüning Era*

The spectacular successes of the NSDAP at the polls in 1930–1 initially paid few dividends to Hitler politically. On the contrary, both at home and abroad fear of the 'fascist menace' was great. This promoted a rallying of the moderate forces and appeared to strengthen the efforts of those who wished to maintain political

1. T. Eschenburg, 'Die europäischen Demokratien zwischen den Weltkriegen', in *Das Dritte Reich und Europa*, Munich 1957.

reason, responsibility and conciliation. The shock of the September elections of 1930 led to the recalling of short-term foreign credits amounting to some 2–3 billion marks, and exacerbated the financial troubles of the public purse and of private enterprise. It was against this background that Brüning achieved some remarkable successes in the spring and summer of 1931 in respect of Germany's foreign debts. Thanks to the intervention of President Herbert Hoover, a one-year moratorium was declared on all future German reparations payments. Two visits by Brüning to London in June and July 1931 moreover yielded an agreement designed to prevent the further flight of capital from Germany. At the end of September the French Minister President Pierre Laval visited Berlin accompanied by Foreign Minister Aristide Briand. This visit provided further proof that Brüning had gained a strong personal prestige in the West, especially in Britain and America which helped his position at home. He had taken energetic steps to stabilise public finances immediately after assuming the chancellorship. And his insistence that the former victorious powers should make concessions also looked reasonable to London and Washington.

However, Brüning also encountered setbacks in his endeavour to cut the ground from under the feet of his Nazi opponents by achieving foreign policy successes which pandered to German nationalism. Thus his idea of a customs union with Austria which he promoted from early 1931 without prior consultation with Britain and France came to grief. It ran into strong opposition in France and finally collapsed, leaving behind a lot of ill-feeling. In May the French recalled their Austrian credits on a massive scale, thereby triggering off the collapse of the *Österreichische Creditanstalt*, by far the largest Viennese bank. This collapse in turn prominently contributed to the bankruptcies of a number of German banks and companies in July 1931. The Reich government could barely control the worst reverberations of this crisis by declaring a bank holiday lasting three weeks and by helping with attempts to rescue the indebted institutions and enterprises. These events undermined the psychological and political gains which Brüning had made through the Hoover Moratorium and the London Agreement. In the summer and autumn of 1931 Brüning issued fresh emergency decrees stipulating cuts in wages and salaries. This gave the

radicals on the extreme Right and Left an opportunity to unleash their demagogy against the 'hunger chancellor' and the
'Weimar system' in general. The 'crisis of capitalism' seemed to
be indisputable, not least because of the massive interventions
which the Brüning Cabinet made in the economy from the
summer of 1931 onwards. These realities created the psychological preconditions which enabled not only the Communists and
Socialists, but also people like Gregor Strasser to talk so con-
vincingly of the 'anti-capitalist longings' that were spreading
among the German population.

Brüning had expected the moderate Right to be strengthened
by the election result. The Nazi victory was therefore a serious
blow to Brüning and his domestic strategy. On 7 October 1930
he had a first conversation with Hitler in the course of which
the Reich Chancellor quickly realised that Hitler was no less
prepared to 'tolerate' his government than was Hugenberg's
DNVP. In view of this Brüning had no choice but to turn to the
Social Democrats and to persuade them to do nothing to overthrow his government (toleration policy). The Nazi victory had
triggered a marked change of atmosphere within the SPD as a
result of which the idea of a defence of the Republic gained
precedence over existing political differences with the Brüning
Cabinet. Consequently there developed a constellation which
promoted a partial collaboration between the Reich Chancellor
and the SPD leadership. This entente received flanking support
from the SPD-led Prussian government which began to take
firm measures against the Nazis within its own area of authority.

The defensive front built up by the republican forces scored a
first success in February 1931 following violent clashes between
Nazis and Communists after the opening of the Reichstag in
October 1930: a majority ratified a change of parliamentary rules
which considerably curtailed both the opportunities for a breach
of procedures in the debating chamber and the misuse of parliamentary immunity by extremist deputies. This caused the
Nazis to withdraw from the Reichstag under noisy protest. They
were followed by the Communists and the DNVP. The NSDAP
absented itself from parliament in subsequent weeks, only to
discover that this response proved self-defeating: a party majority stretching from the moderate Left (SPD) to the moderate

Right (Conservative People's Party) continued to exist and to support Brüning. In fact, this majority decided to suspend parliamentary proceedings until October 1931 to assist Brüning's attempts to tackle the crisis.

Meanwhile the campaigns to discredit the Republic and its organs which the Nazis launched at different levels met with repeated success. Goebbels's agitation of November 1930 against *All Quiet on the Western Front* offers a case in point. On the other hand, such activities were not conducive to bringing Hitler closer to a conquest of power. The system of government by presidential decree eroded the influence of the parties and of the Reichstag. But it also appeared to provide a palliative against demagogic mass movements. Since the autumn of 1930 people had become more conscious of the need to put up defences against the National Socialists. This response took different forms. The Republican paramilitary organisation, the *Reichsbanner*, stepped up its recruitment and its rallies; the Catholic bishops issued stern warnings against Nazism; the state governments published decrees ordering more vigorous countermeasures against political violence. All these counteractions induced Hitler repeatedly to remind the NSDAP and the SA in the course of 1931 of the need to maintain discipline. On 1 April 1931 the party suffered a double blow when the Berlin SA staged the Stennes Rebellion and Frick was ousted from the Thuringian government. The setbacks demonstrated that, its successful mass propaganda notwithstanding, the party faced a dilemma of some proportion and had to guard against being thrown once more into the political ghetto of radicalism.

These developments also limited the chances of Hitler, Göring and other prominent Nazi leaders to win successes in negotiations with the *Reichswehr* and the conservative elites in business and agriculture. They had divided among themselves the task of improving relations with these circles and of mobilising them against the Brüning government. Thus in 1930–1 the support afforded by large-scale industry to the Nazis remained restricted to a few personal contacts. Else Bruckmann, Hitler's supporter in Munich, had put him into touch with the Octogenarian Emil Kirdorf, the Director General of the *Gelsenkirchener Bergwerks-A.G.* as early as 1927. Kirdorf had a long standing reputation as a radical Pan-German and was an outsider among the Ruhr industrialists. In 1930–1 new and important links were forged above all to Hjalmar Schacht and the Düsseldorf tycoon Fritz Thyssen who was involved with the *Vereinigte Stahlwerke*. Thyssen *inter alia* gave money to the conversion of the 'Brown House' in Munich. He also paid considerable sums to Göring who was thought to represent the pro-industry faction in the NSDAP. Göring also succeeded in winning over Ludwig Grauert, the General Secretary (*Syndikus*) of the North-West German Association of Heavy Industrial Employers' organisations, as well as Walter Funk, an economics editor from Berlin. Grauert became State Secretary in the Prussian Ministry of the Interior in 1933; Funk succeeded Schacht as Reich Economics Minister in 1939.

But for most of big business and its peak association, the *Reichsverband der deutschen Industrie* (RDI), the NSDAP did not become a desirable partner which deserved financial and political support even after its 1930 electoral success. It was only in 1931–2 that this attitude underwent a slow change. This is reflected in the invitation issued to Hitler to address the prestigious Düsseldorf *Industrieklub* on 26 January 1932; it is also reflected in the founding of a 'Working Office' which Schacht, Paul Reusch, the Director General of the *Gutehoffnungshütte*, and others promoted in the spring of 1932 as a way of advising the NSDAP in matters of economic policy. In parallel with this office emerged the 'Keppler Circle' to which belonged prominent industrialists like Albert Vögler (*Vereinigte Stahlwerke*), the Berlin bankers Friedrich Reinhart and Emil Meyer, the Cologne banker Kurt von Schröder, and Emil Helfferich and F.A. Witthoeft, two wealthy wholesalers from Hamburg.

However, from the NSDAP's point of view large donations and the 'big shots' in industry and commerce were less important from 1930–1 onwards than the many small and often anonymous contributions by local notables. These contributions began to flow more generously once the Nazis had won their electoral victories and it was no longer inconceivable that they might assume government responsibility. As in Munich, Hitler also found wealthy men and women in Berlin who opened doors for him in high society. Viktoria von Dircksen, a naïve admirer of the *Führer*, was particularly active in this respect. She was nicknamed 'Hitler Mummy' among Nazis in Berlin and frequently hosted Hitler, Göring and Goebbels at her Berlin town house.

Other factors also boosted the social prestige of the Nazi movement. Thus August Wilhelm von Preussen, a son of the Kaiser, joined the party in the spring of 1931. From 1931 onwards Hitler also made it his habit to reside at the famous *Kaiserhof* Hotel, opposite the Reich Chancellery, when he came to Berlin. This may have increased his respectability in the eyes of the public. But for the time being it did not enhance the *Führer's* chances of gaining a hold in the government. Thus a plebiscite to dissolve the Prussian Diet prematurely, which had been initiated by the *Stahlhelm* ex-Servicemen's Association and the DNVP and to which the Nazis had given their vehement support, failed on 9 August 1931. The intended removal of the Social Democratic Prussian government had thus been prevented.

Close co-operation between Otto Braun's Prussian government which had the support of the Catholic Centre Party and Brüning's Cabinet could have formed the most important plank for a stabilisation of the Weimar Republic. It was Braun who soon after the 1930 elections raised the question of a link-up of the Reich government with the Prussian government. He saw it as a contribution to the long-debated reform of the Reich constitution and as a means of nationalising and simplifying the bureaucratic apparatus. However, both the Reich President and the *Reichswehr* showed no interest in this plan. Members of the Cabinet shared the aversion against the SPD-led Prussian government whose removal had been on the 'shopping list of Hindenburg's old friends' since the spring of 1930.[2] These attitudes fatefully contributed to the fact that the opportunities for stabilising the Republic were not sufficiently exploited and even undermined. For years the relationship between the President and the Prussian government had been under considerable strain over a number of issues. Among these were the secret rearmament plans of the *Reichswehr* and the *Osthilfe* programme of economic aid for the East Elbian landowners. Fresh tensions with Braun arose in June 1930 when Hindenburg signalled that he would only attend the celebrations to be held in connection with the French evacuation of the rest of the Rhineland, if the

2. H. Schulze, op.cit., pp. 627f.

Prussian government lifted its ban on the Rhenish branch of the
Stahlhelm. This regional organisation had been outlawed in 1929
after engaging in illegal military training exercises. The conflict
also revealed that, when put on the spot, Brüning would be
more likely to comply with Hindenburg's wishes than to side
with the Prussian government. Brüning was further drawn into
the Hindenburg camp in the summer of 1931, a few days before
the plebiscite for the dissolution of the Prussian Diet. This
particular dispute stemmed from a presidential emergency decree of 17 July 1931, initiated by the Braun government and
designed to deal with political violence. Braun now argued that
this decree was to be employed in equal measure against both
right-wing and left-wing extremism. Hindenburg who saw himself as the protector of the *Stahlhelm* was very annoyed by this
interpretation. All this meant that the failure of the plebiscite did
not result in an improvement of relations. On the contrary, the
atmosphere 'between the two sides of the *Wilhelmstrasse*' remained 'extremely frosty'.[3]

Above all, the balance of power between the Reich and the
states shifted increasingly towards the central government. In
particular, the emergency decrees of the summer and autumn
1931 interfered with the fiscal rights of the *Länder*. The Prussian
government's response was, *inter alia*, to refuse any further
involvement in the *Osthilfe* programme and to withdraw from
this particular battle-ground. Conscious of his political responsibility, Braun moreover tried to put to positive use the erosion of
Prussia's power position *vis-à-vis* the Reich. Thus he hinted at
the beginning of November 1931 that he might be prepared to
resign if Brüning became the successor and combined the post
of Reich Chancellor and Minister President. Such a combination
would no doubt have strengthened Brüning's position *vis-à-vis*
Hindenburg's and opened up fresh possibilities for stabilising
the Republic. In his postwar memoirs Brüning called Braun's
proposal a plan of 'greatest importance' adding: 'As Reich
Chancellor I could be dismissed by the Reich President, but not
so as Prussian Minister President. All the events of the summer
of 1931 [ending in Brüning's dismissal] . . . could have been
prevented'. However, Hindenburg declared categorically that

3. Ibid., p. 670.

he would 'never find such a proposal acceptable'.[4] Evidently the President had been told that the Chancellor's dependence on him and hence presidential power would be tangibly reduced. The phalanx of particularist interest which had Hindenburg's ear lightly brushed aside the need to prop up the Republic which ought to have been the primary consideration.

The gap between the Reich and Prussia was further widened in the course of 1931 as a result of differing assessments of the Nazi threat. Guided by Severing and his staunchly republican Under-Secretary of State Otto Abegg, the Prussian Ministry of the Interior had issued a decree on 30 July 1930 postulating that holding a civil or public service position was incompatible with membership of the anti-republican NSDAP and KPD. It was a maxim to which the Prussian government adhered up to 20 July 1932, when it was forcibly removed from office. A similar directive existed for the army since 1927 where it was even more important that it should be adhered to. Groener had reaffirmed this position on 6 October 1930 after three young lieutenants had been sentenced at Leipzig on grounds of Nazi activity. He had no doubt, he said, 'that officers who held such views could not remain in the armed forces'.[5]

But soon the *Reichswehr* Ministry began to diverge from this principle. Schleicher, Groener's political adviser, began to mastermind more and more persistent inquiries addressed to the Reich Chancellor and the Reich Ministry of the Interior querying the assumption that the Nazi movement was a subversive party and that public servants could hence not be members of the NSDAP or SA. The *Reichswehr* leadership pointed in particular to the legality oath that Hitler had sworn in connection with the Leipzig officers' trials. It was also mentioned that Brüning had meanwhile had a conversation with Hitler and that a Nazi had become Minister of the Interior in Thuringia. But underlying this change of heart was the naive satisfaction felt by high-ranking officers that Hitler had explicitly (and with *Reichswehr* feelings on this point very much in mind) supported the idea of strong armaments and a 'spiritual' military preparedness (*Wehrgedanke*). Moreover there was the growing desire on the

4. H. Brüning, *Memoiren, 1978–1934*, Stuttgart 1970, pp. 247f
5. I. Maurer and U. Wengst (eds.), *Staat und NSDAP, 1930–1932. Quellen zur Ära Brüning*, Düsseldorf 1977, pp. 159f.

part of the officer corps to use SA- and *Stahlhelm*-members and others who had received a paramilitary training, as reinforcements of the border protection contingents in the east. They also hoped that some day the paramilitary associations might be deployed as a militia to back up the 100,000 men *Reichwehr* and hence be put more closely under *Reichswehr* control. Since the spring of 1931 Röhm and Hitler had been paying visits to Schleicher, Groener and Hans von Hammerstein-Equord, the chief of the *Heeresleitung*. On 10 October 1931 Hitler then had his first audience with Hindenburg. All these contacts were designed to underline the allegedly legal aims of the Nazi movement and to complain about the discriminations against the NSDAP which were said to be unjustified. Slowly the *Reichswehr* leadership was gaining ground *vis-à-vis* the politicians who remained suspicious of Nazi protestations. All this happened against the background of an unprecedented rise in political violence in which Nazis and Communists began to outdo each other. In November 1931, then, police and state prosecutor in Hesse found firm evidence of plans to mobilise the SA in case of a *coup d'état*. These 'Boxheim Documents' revealed that the idea of a violent seizure of power had by no means been dropped and was particularly ingrained in the SA.

This did not prevent Groener from declaring, in a revised decree of 29 January 1932, that the *Reichswehr* would in future be open to 'every German who had not been proven to have been a participant in activities designed to overthrow the Republic'. The only exception were members of parties 'which, like the Communist Party, base their programme on a revolutionary attitude and permanent hostility to the existing order'. As far as other parties were concerned which similarly may have posed a threat to the constitution, it should be borne in mind, Groener concluded, that they could have changed their position.[6] This was a barely veiled rejection of the principle that right-wing and left-wing extremists were to be given equal treatment. The *Reichswehr* Ministry reneged on its earlier directive which stipulated the exclusion of Nazis from the armed forces. This was also how the decree of January 1932 was interpreted in public. Like the Prussian government, the interior ministers of the south

6. Ibid., pp. 276ff.

German states regarded this decree as a sign of weakness and unjustified leniency. They criticised the new policy all the more vigorously after Groener, in addition to the *Reichwehr* Ministry, had taken over the Reich Ministry of the Interior in October 1931. What they feared was that thenceforth similar principles might also be applied to the police and the bureaucracy in general.

Some six weeks before the publication of Groener's decree of 29 January 1932 it had once more become clear how wide the gap between the army leadership and the Prussian government had grown in respect of their assessments of the Nazi movement. Hitler, spending a few days at the Berlin *Kaiserhof* and posing as the up-and-coming man had pompously invited the 'gentlemen of the foreign press' to a conference scheduled for 11 December 1931. Grzesinski, who had always been an advocate of drastic measures to combat Nazi challenges, proposed that the press conference be banned by the Prussian police and that Hitler, who still held Austrian citizenship, should be deported from Prussian territory. Severing, too, thought it intolerable that Hitler was trying 'to set up a new shop opposite the Reich Chancellery' and that he should be allowed freely to hold court at the *Kaiserhof*.[7] However, the Prussian government had to abandon its plan. Hitler's deportation would have required the approval of the Reich government, and the Reich Chancellery signalled that it was not prepared to give its support to Grzesinski's proposal.

Consequently this last attempt failed to keep the Nazi Party away from the power-centre of the Reich. Ten weeks later Hitler was made a *Regierungsrat* in the State of Brunswick where a fellow Nazi, Dietrich Klagges, occupied the Ministry of the Interior. This civil service rank automatically gave Hitler German citizenship. Thenceforth it was no longer possible to deport him. Above all, the move created the legal prerequisites of Hitler's nomination as a candidate in the impending elections of a new Reich President called for March 1932.

Of course, chances of Hitler being elected to the presidency were not particularly good. Moreover, his candidacy was bound to put him into direct competition with Hindenburg and the

7. Ibid., pp. 266ff.

forces backing him, not least the army leadership which he had wooed as eagerly in the months before. The move must therefore be seen as an attempt to escape from the *cul-de-sac* into which his unsuccessful earlier manoeuvres to gain executive power had led him. In the autumn of 1931 the downfall of the Reich government seemed to be just around the corner, but the opportunity was missed. Since the bank crash of July 1931 Brüning had taken energetic measures to stem the crisis. But this could not prevent a weakening of and a loss of confidence in, his government among the public, among the *Reichswehr* leaders and, to some extent, in industry and the DVP. Governing without parliament for months on end, Brüning's style of government had become increasingly semi-dictatorial and bureaucratic-authoritarian. He allied himself with two or three dozen ministers, top civil servants and a few experts, and from the peak of the crisis in the summer of 1931 became more and more intolerant of criticisms voiced by the parties, the lobbies and the states. He was convinced that these criticisms were secondary in comparison to the objective pressures (*Sachzwänge*) to which his policy was subject. He was increasingly inclined to expose the population to ever greater restrictions confident that there was no alternative to persistence and 'tunnelling through the hump' in the spirit of an austere Prussianism. And as criticism of his policies mounted, he remained unwavering about those policies' wisdom and morality. What was to lead to his downfall in May 1932 were not only the intrigues of the *Reichswehr* leadership and other lobbies around the Reich President, but also the uncharismatic inflexibility of his conduct. Finally, Brüning also became a captive of the calculations and priorities which he had laid down himself in the fields of foreign and economic policy.

One of Brüning's *idées fixes* was his conviction that public finances could only be put in order again, if the country went through a longer period of utmost parsimony and public expenditure cuts. For him this strategy was a prerequisite of foreign policy successes. In the field of diplomacy he gave first priority to the complete cancellation of reparations once the Hoover Moratorium had expired. After the start of the Geneva disarmament negotiations in February 1932 he, moreover, aimed at the re-establishment of military equality for Germany. In order to undercut his right-wing nationalist opponents, he gave plenty of advance publicity of the official German position. But this publicity tended to damage his negotiating plank, especially *vis-à-vis* France. Thus it contributed to the Lausanne Conference (which was to bring about a final settlement of the reparations question) being postponed until June 1932. By that time, however, Brüning had lost his chancellorship.

The primacy of foreign policy considerations also explains in good measure the inflexibility which Brüning displayed in his policy of economic stabilisation. In the autumn of 1931 the economic crisis also hit Britain, France and the United States with increasing severity. There were bank crashes and many companies were forced into liquidation. Britain devalued the pound and abandoned the gold standard in order to stabilise her currency. These developments led to Brüning's strategy being reinforced by the expectation that Germany would be able to gain a competitive advantage in exports over the Western industrial nations, if she did not waver from her deflationary financial policy and the forcible reduction of wages and prices at home. This in turn would reduce the country's financial and political dependence on the West and facilitate a successful revision of the Versailles Treaty. Seen with the benefit of hindsight, such high hopes which codetermined Brüning's austerity decrees of October and December 1931 would appear to have been based on a very unfortunate overestimation of foreign policy priorities over social welfare at home. Since the end of 1931 demands could be heard in the German public to tackle the crisis with the help of public works programmes and a productive deficit spending policy. Both the Free Trade Unions and some Nazis promoted ideas to this effect which were later successfully put into practice both in the United States and in Germany. But the priorities which Brüning had laid down contributed to such alternatives not being seriously considered in his time. Nor were his policies able to halt the depression and mass unemployment until his dismissal in May 1932. This is why his period of office bears the odium of unsuccessful or misguided crisis management.

From the autumn of 1931, the Germans became increasingly aware of the futility of Brüning's policy. To be sure, this was not least the result of the agitation by the radicals on the extreme

105

Right and Left of the political spectrum. But if the capacity of large parts of the population to bear with a government which acted imperviously to, and remotely from, public sentiments was much weaker than Brüning had assumed, this was not merely due to Nazi and Communist demagogy.

In the autumn of 1931 the political intrigues against the Reich Chancellor only just failed to topple him. What helped to save him was the prestige which he still enjoyed at that time in influential circles, especially among the experts in the ministerial bureaucracy. The *Reichswehr* and Schleicher in particular accused Brüning of being too dependent on the Social Democrats and the trade union lobby within his Catholic Centre Party. After the final collapse of the plans for a German–Austrian customs union, Julius Curtius, the Foreign Minister, lost the confidence of his own party, the right-of-centre DVP. Brüning was forced to sacrifice at the same time his Reich Minister of the Interior, Joseph Wirth, who was reckoned to belong to the left wing of the Centre Party. These manoeuvres raised the question of whether the Brüning Cabinet would be able to survive. The Chancellor quickly changed his Cabinet, putting Groener, in addition to the *Reichswehr* Ministry, in Wirth's place and taking over the Foreign Ministry himself. In this way he succeeded in forestalling the more far-reaching plans of his opponents, the more so as the swap left the *Reichswehr* leadership in the comfortable assumption that it had increased its influence on the government.

Nevertheless, the criticisms which had been mounting in right-wing circles, the DVP and the *Wirtschaftspartei* included, continued to smoulder for many weeks. The opening of parliament after the summer recess had been set for 13 October 1931, and the right-wing opposition expected to win a vote of no-confidence in Brüning. Hectic behind-the-scenes negotiations took place concerning a possible alternative government. One of the alternatives mooted was a straight-forwardly right-wing cabinet which would include the Nazis. Hindenburg's reception of Hitler on 10 October was designed to explore this possibility. Furthermore, Hugenberg and his friends in the *Stahlhelm* leadership initiated a big rally of all right-wing opponents of Brüning at Bad Harzburg. Staged before the opening of the Reichstag it became known as the Harzburg Front.

The Harzburg rally of all prominent right-wing nationalist politicians which also featured the former *Reichsbank* President, Schacht, among its speakers was not a genuine success. After heated arguments within its own ranks, the RDI, industry's peak association, could not bring itself to appear in public at Bad Harzburg despite its severe doubts about Brüning's policies. Above all, there was Hitler's long-standing and openly expressed aversion to show himself on the same platform with the 'sclerotic' excellencies and privy councillors around Hugenberg. This aversion became once more apparent at Harzburg and in a most provocative fashion: first he arrived deliberately late; he then made a more or less surly speech in front of the assembled right-wing notables and finally he left the scene straight after the march past of the SA and without waiting for the columns of the *Stahlhelm* that followed the Brownshirts. At a subsequent SA rally in the city of Brunswick, the *Führer* made his point even more clearly: he wanted to rely first and foremost on his own supporters.

The disunity of the 'National Opposition' stood in marked contrast to the passionate statement which Brüning made in defence of his policies before the Reichstag on 13 October. Above all, it also ruined his opponents' plan to pass a vote of no confidence in him. When the votes were counted on 16 October, Brüning, contrary to many people's expectations, gained a slim majority of twenty-five. He obtained the solid support of the Centre Party, the SPD and the DDP. But he also succeeded in keeping the small *Wirtschaftspartei* on his side. The DVP with its links with industry made a pitiful showing: some of its deputies voted for, others against Brüning, while a third group either stayed at home or abstained from the vote.

As a result of these developments, the Nazi leadership also changed its attitude towards the Reich Chancellor. On 13 December Hitler wrote him an open letter in which he found, next to sharp criticisms, also special words of respect. The letter indicated that there existed within the NSDAP strong forces which seriously thought of linking up with the Centre Party instead of remaining in the fragile Harzburg Front. These forces were represented above all by Gregor Strasser; they hoped that the NSDAP would achieve a share in the government more quickly by this route. Brüning had several conversations with

Strasser in this period and, if only for tactical reasons, contributed to keeping this alternative open. The idea received a fresh boost after the elections for the Hessian Diet in November 1931 when negotiations began between the Centre Party and the NSDAP aiming to replace the Social Democratic government at Darmstadt.

As late as January 1932, Brüning was working on the assumption that Hitler, following the failure of the Harzburg Front to seize power, would prefer to seek a rapprochement with the existing government. At least, he thought, the Nazi leader would avoid a renewed sharp conflict with the Chancellor and the President. He therefore also believed that Hitler could be won over to a plan concerning the future of Hindenburg. The idea was to get the Reichstag to approve a change of the Constitution aimed at extending Hindenburg's term of office without another popular election. But Hugenberg's DNVP refused to support this idea. Consequently Hitler, who did not wish to be outdone by Hugenberg in his radical opposition, also turned Brüning's approaches down. The negotiations between the Centre Party and the NSDAP in Hesse now also came to nought. After a longer period of procrastination Hitler finally allowed himself to be proclaimed as candidate for the presidential elections on 13 March 1932. Goebbels made the announcement on 22 February at a rally in the Berlin *Sportpalast* after a last-minute attempt to agree on a joint candidate with the rest of the 'National Opposition' had petered out. Hugenberg and the *Stahlhelm* put up their own candidate, the *Stahlhelm* leader Theodor Duesterberg. The Communists had already announced that Ernst Thälmann, their chief executive, would also stand. Much to his chagrin, Hindenburg was therefore once more dependent on the forces supporting Brüning, if he wanted to win the elections, and these forces of course included the Social Democrats. The SPD, selflessly and moved by *raison d'état*, energetically lobbied for the old Field Marshal as the 'lesser evil'. But above all it was thanks to Brüning's relentless campaigning, if it proved possible to present Hindenburg as the alleged guardian of the Constitution to a front ranging from the moderate Left to the moderate Right.

And yet, paradoxical as it may seem, it was this peculiar constellation which lay at the root of the later 'ingratitude' shown by the 'old gentleman' towards his chancellor. Hindenburg was deeply angered that Brüning had not succeeded in getting at least Hugenberg and the *Stahlhelm* to support his re-election. Instead the President was forced to rely on political forces, above all the Catholics and the SPD, about which he had the gravest reservations in view of his own background and outlook upon the world. But the Weimar constitutional order had long ceased to be a parliamentary republic. Constitutional reality had meanwhile become orientated towards a single person, the octogenarian Paul von Hindenburg. It was these realities which turned the President's highly personal sentiments into a political factor of major proportions, the more so as his feelings could be easily influenced by people who had his ear. Brüning and large sections of the liberal press had portrayed the ageing Field Marshal as the strongest and allegedly neutral bastion of republicanism. They had done so to prevent worse from happening and often against their better judgement. But now, after the election, the fallacies of this self-denying ordinance became clear.

The developments of the spring of 1932 must also be seen in the following broader context. Unlike in 1925, no one in the SPD and the Centre Party then even vaguely thought of putting up a convincing and reliable republican as a candidate of the middle ground and in lieu of the old Hindenburg. This mission seems to demonstrate how far the preceding collapse of parliamentary government since 1930 had pushed the democratic parties into a position of inner resignation. Thus the weakness of the Republic was reflected in the fatalism of the republican parliamentary forces which could still have formed a majority. In the spring of 1932 this Republic entered its final phase before the Nazi seizure of power in January 1923.

Carried away by their own campaign, the Nazis increasingly convinced themselves in the early days of March that Hitler could win the presidential elections. Goebbels had pushed Hitler hardest to challenge Hindenburg and had repeatedly been critical of the *Führer*'s dithering. But now he became worried that the Nazi Party machine was growing over-optimistic. Thus he noted on 6 March 1932: 'The estimates in our favour are reaching fantastic proportions'.[8] As late as election day, on 13

8. J. Goebbels, *Vom Kaiserhof zur Reichskanzlei*, Berlin 1934, pp. 57ff.

March, he registered that a 'victorious mood' prevailed 'everywhere'. But great disappointment set in less than twenty-four hours later: 'We have been beaten', Goebbels wrote, ' . . . our members we are in a state of deep depression and dejection . . . By 2 a.m. we were rudely shaken out of the dream of [obtaining] power, at least for the time being'.

Hindenburg just missed the absolute majority. He gained 49.6 per cent. Hitler won no more than 30.1 per cent. The result was worse than what the Nazis had achieved in most of the preceding regional elections. Thälmann, who obtained 13.2 per cent and Duesterberg who scored 6.8 per cent were even further behind. There were rumours of a Nazi Putsch in the event of a Hitler victory and, as searches by the police of SA homes in Berlin on the eve of the poll showed, there was some truth in these rumours. It is possible that these discoveries cost Hitler some votes.

The police investigations in Berlin and elsewhere moreover led to the maturing of a decision by the interior ministries of the Reich and the States to ban the SA and thereby to put a determined stop to the Brownshirts' dangerous and subversive activities. Groener, who wished to regain his reputation as a strong man after his *Reichswehr* decree of February 1932 which had been so lenient towards the Nazis, now favoured a ban. So did Schleicher. All one was waiting for was the end of the second ballot on 10 April which had become necessary after the inconclusive outcome of the presidential elections in March. The Nazis were not to be given an opportunity to present themselves as martyrs of state oppression. Duesterberg dropped out of this second poll, enabling Hindenburg to attract 53 per cent of the vote. Hitler increased his support to 36.8 per cent, with Thälmann trailing behind at 10.2 per cent. Three days later, on 13 April 1932, Brüning issued a decree, signed by Hindenbrug, banning the SA and the SS in order 'to secure the authority of the state'. The promoters of the decree knew that the ban was more a political demonstration without much significance from a policing point of view. Like the Communists, the Nazis had long learned to circumvent such bans by adopting cunning camouflages which, to make matters worse, deliberately tended to mock the authorities. What in the final analysis represented the most important aspect of the SA ban was that the authorities had made it clear that they were prepared to defend themselves against growing attempts at intimidation by the Nazis.

On the other hand, the ban had come about in circumstances which did not augur well for the unity of purpose with which the Reich government was prepared to pursue its defensive policies. There existed serious qualms among the upper ranks of the *Reichswehr* which did not like to disturb its now more relaxed relationship with the SA. This led Schleicher to change his attitude after 9 April. Unlike his minister, Groener, he did not advocate proscription anymore in the decisive discussion in the Cabinet and subsequently with Hindenburg prior to the publication of the ban. Rather he recommended that Hitler should be handed an ultimatum demanding a restructuring of the SA. The aim of this reorganisation would be to do away with the SA's 'military character which posed a danger to the State'.[9] Another argument used in *Reichswehr* circles was that a ban on the SA should be accompanied by a dissolution of the mainly Social-Democratic and republican paramilitary organisation, the *Reichsbanner*. Schleicher failed to get his way in the Cabinet. Nor was the idea of an ultimatum practical enough to convince the Reich President. However, his arguments caused Hindenburg to waver. In the end he could only bring himself to sign the SA decree after Groener and Brüning had threatened to resign, if he did not. For the first time and in the name of the *Reichswehr* Schleicher had therefore openly objected to a decision by the Reich government. He had dissociated himself from Groener, 'his paternal friend', who acted as Minister of the Interior in this matter and, in particular, had to take account of the views of the police forces in the states.

What moved this 'political general' were not merely the narrow interests of the *Reichswehr* bureaucracy. He looked beyond the *Reichswehr*-SA relationship and for several months now had been aiming to integrate the Nazis into a new Cabinet which would be more right-wing than the Brüning government. Hindenburg was basically in agreement with him over this matter. The ban on the SA did not fit into this political programme. Schleicher also cherished the illusion that he would succeed in putting Hitler on a tight lead. What he did not take sufficient

9. T. Vogelsang, *Reichswehr, Staat und NSDAP*, Stuttgart 1962, p. 170.

account of was that the Nazis had once more been shunted into a political *cul-de-sac* thanks to the proclaimed willingness of the authorities to defend the existing order. This meant that, if the authority of the State was to be upheld, the spring of 1932 was not a time to help the Hitler movement escape from its dilemma.

However, Schleicher willy-nilly provided precisely this help when after the proclamation of the SA ban he stepped up his efforts to engineer the downfall of the Brüning Cabinet. Through intermediaries — among them the Berlin SA leader Wolf Count Helldorf and Werner von Alvensleben, an intriguer and friend of Schleicher's — Röhm and Hitler learned very quickly what the *Reichswehr* leadership thought of the ban. They were also informed of Hindenburg's rapidly growing qualms about the alleged 'one-sidedness' of this decree. As early as 15 April Hindenburg wrote a distinctly cool letter to Groener. In it he told Groener that the same objections about violent behaviour which had been levelled against the SA could also be raised against the *Reichsbanner*. He would therefore have to ask Groener to examine the available material 'with the same seriousness' as had been applied during the preparation of the SA ban.[10] Although the evidence against the *Reichsbanner* was thin, it is clear that Hindenburg was annoyed. To some extent this was also Groener's fault. He was torn between the right-wing officer corps, on the one hand, and the representatives of the Reich Ministry of the Interior most of whom were still solidly republican, on the other. This as well as personal reasons had undermined his determination and ability to give a firm lead during a decisive phase of Weimar politics. It resulted in his contradictory policy which vacillated between the lenient *Reichswehr* decree of February and the SA ban in April. Ultimately he found himself sitting between all political stools. He began to lose Hindenburg's long-standing confidence and became the target of very harsh criticisms by the entire nationalist Right.

In the second half of April Brüning was tied down by the disarmament negotiations at Geneva. He also held talks with the French Minister President André Tardieu, which he had long been hoping for. At the end of the month he returned without having won a tangible success and found that the

10. Ibid., p. 177.

political climate in Berlin had dramatically changed in his disfavour. His opponents had succeeded in convincing Hindenburg that the Reich Chancellor was the main obstacle to shifting the government towards the Right. On 30 April Brüning had a conversation with the President at which Hindenburg's belief emerged more clearly than before. Again the Field Marshal raised the question of the SA ban and of 'equal treatment' for the *Reichsbanner*. There was also the important factor of the results of the Prussian Diet elections on 24 April. As anticipated, the ruling Weimar coalition of SPD, Centre Party and DDP lost its majority on this occasion. This opened up the opportunity for the Catholics to participate in a newly formed right-wing coalition. Hindenburg expected Brüning to influence his Centre Party colleagues in this direction. But contrary to the views of some of its right-wing representatives, Franz von Papen among them, the Prussian Catholics maintained a position of cautious attention which made it possible for Braun to remain in office as caretaker. But in matters of Reich politics Brüning was not particularly accommodating either. He told Hindenburg on 30 April that it would be better to wait 'until after Lausanne' to effect the much-vaunted right-wing shift in the Cabinet, if only to avoid a hardening of the French attitude in the impending important diplomatic negotiations. Brüning thought, wrongly, as it turned out, that his energetic support of Hindenburg's re-election campaign had committed the President to his policies for at least some time. This is why he displayed in these last weeks of his chancellorship a stubbornness in the pursuit of his domestic and foreign policies which people had not experienced before then. He clung firmly to the 'objective tasks' still to be solved. But in the process he lost almost completely his capacity to deploy political countermeasures against the intrigues which had meanwhile been started against him.

On 26 April Schleicher had received Hitler for an exchange of views. He tried to find out how the *Führer* would react to the formation of a new cabinet on the assumption that the SA ban would be lifted. Another meeting between the two took place on 7 May. On this occasion Hitler was given an assurance that he would be able to see Hindenburg. It appears that Schleicher had made contact with Papen even before his meetings with the Nazi leader. Both men knew each other from their spell on the

General Staff during the First World War. Papen had risen within the Westphalian Centre Party and acted as a spokesman of agrarian organisations in the Prussian Diet. Being a dashing 'gentleman horseback rider', he looked to Schleicher as the ideal replacement for Brüning, combining, as he did, agrarian concerns with military experience and conservative ideas with Centre Party membership. The scheming general does not appear to have been too worried about the fact that the Catholics could not possibly be prepared to regard a conservative maverick like Papen as their representative after Brüning's downfall.

On 9 May the Reichstag reconvened for a few days to consider the budget and to listen to a defence of the SA ban by Groener. But faced with a barrage of abuse from the Nazis, the Minister cut a very poor figure. Now even Count Westarp and other moderate Conservatives were up in arms over him. Schleicher, too, spoke out against his superior. On 12 May Groener saw no alternative but to resign. The dismantling of the Brüning Cabinet had begun. For the first time and mainly through Schleicher, the Nazis were included in the preliminary discussions for the formation of a new cabinet. Various plans were mooted and by the end of May a list of new ministers had been compiled, while Hindenburg spent some time on his *Neudeck* estate in East Prussia. Travelling to *Neudeck* on 28 May, his State Secretary Meissner submitted to the President the draft of another emergency decree which Brüning had prepared. This decree envisaged the carving up of those East Elbian estates which had no hope of ever overcoming their indebtedness. The agrarian mafia around Hindenburg had been arguing long before this that this was a Bolshevik measure intended to initiate the expropriation of the landowners. Briefed in this fashion, Hindenburg refused to receive Brüning personally at *Neudeck*. Instead his State Secretary acted as the messenger boy.

On the following day, Hindenburg returned to Berlin and Brüning asked for an immediate audience. He was again informed about what Meissner had already told him: the President was not prepared to sign this emergency decree. In fact his refusal was no more than an excuse for the Chancellor's dismissal which had been decided upon beforehand. Perhaps the President was moved by feelings of guilt when, towards the end of the audience, he said curtly and in a manner calculated to

114

hurt Brüning that, if he wished to see him again on the following day, he should come along with his letter of resignation in his pocket. When Brüning reappeared with his letter on 30 May his resignation was immediately accepted. But, although deeply offended by the treatment he had received at the hands of the President, the Chancellor maintained his calm posture of respectful politeness. He did not confront Hindenburg with the irresponsible intrigues which the letter had permitted and even encouraged behind the Chancellor's back.

Goebbels was jubilant on this day:[11] 'The bomb has gone off. Brüning has handed to the Reich President the resignation of the entire Cabinet at noon [today]. The [Weimar] System is on its way towards collapse . . . I drive out to Nauen to meet the *Führer* on his way [to Berlin] from Mecklenburg. . . . The Reich President wants to see him in the course of the afternoon. . . . The conversation with the Reich President has gone well. The SA ban will be lifted; the Reichstag [is to be] dissolved'.

3.2. *The Final Phase and the Destruction of the Republic under Papen*

Not only the National Socialists, but also other contemporaries regarded Brüning's dismissal and the appointment of Papen as a decisive caesura on the Nazi path to power. In his statement of 4 June the new Reich Chancellor pompously spoke of the 'new state' and the 'new Germany' which it was his aim to create. In view of these announcements the supporters of Brüning had good reason to feel, with ex-State Secretary, Hermann Pünder, that the new Cabinet was a 'first stage of the Third Reich'.[12] The Catholics in particular were livid with indignation about the 'traitor' Papen. The latter had assured the leader of the Centre Party, Dr Ludwig Kaas, shortly before Brüning's fall that he would not assume the chancellorship. But on 2 June he quickly changed his mind and was merely able to cover up his about-face by returning his Centre Party membership card. The Centre

11. J. Goebbels, *Kaiserhof*, p. 104.
12. Thus the record in the diary of Hans Schäffer, the State Secretary in the Reich Finance Ministry, for 2 June 1932, after a conversation with Pünder. A copy of the diary is kept in the archive of the *Institut für Zeitgeschichte* in Munich.

Party Reichstag faction published a statement in which it used extraordinarily blunt words criticising the 'irresponsible intrigues of persons who had no constitutional mandate' for their actions and for having engineered the change of government.[13]

Meeting Hindenburg on 30 May, the SPD leaders Otto Wels and Rudolf Breitscheid expressed their fears with regard to the Prussian position. They believed that, 'as the situation unfolded, violations of the Constitution might occur'.[14] They explained that the new government could not expect 'toleration' from the Social Democrats. The executive of the *Staatspartei*, in a letter to the Reich President, indignantly denied that the Papen Cabinet could legitimately call itself a 'government of national concentration'. 'The overwhelming majority of the $19\frac{1}{2}$ million Germans', they added, 'who only a few weeks ago set all party-political considerations aside and decided to support your re-election as Reich President, have no representative in this new cabinet'.[15]

Apart from the Nazis, only the DNVP and the DVP which had drafted further and further towards the Right came out in support of Papen. However, Hugenberg did not conceal his scepticism about the support which the Nazis had promised. He told Hindenburg that 'Hitler would probably change his attitude after the national elections'.[16] Finally, the new government received applause from the extra-parliamentary forces on the Right, in particular from the *Stahlhelm*, the *Reichslandbund* and large sections of industry.

His concessions to the *Reichswehr* and the agrarians notwithstanding, so long as Brüning was in office together with Adam Stegerwald, the Reich Labour Minister and a former Christian trade unionist, or with Hans Schlange-Schöningen, the *Ostkommissar* and member of the People's Conservative Party, all of whom were seriously concerned to maintain a social and political consensus in the face of their austerity programme, the presidential system could still claim to be a trustee of the Republic and thus gain legitimation for its actions. During this

13. Quoted in E. Eyck, op.cit., p. 486.
14. Note by the State Secretary, Meissner, after conversations between party leaders and Hindenburg on 30/31.5.1932. Copy in archive of the *Institut für Zeitgeschichte* in Munich.
15. Thus the two leaders of the *Staatspartei*, August Weber and O. Meyer, in their letter to Hindenburg of 1.6.1932. Copy in the archive of the *Institut für Zeitgeschichte* in Munich.
16. Note by Meissner (see above, note 7).

period there was also a rationale behind the policy of 'toleration' adopted by the Social Democrats, not least because it was designed to block a Nazi assumption of power. But now that the Papen Cabinet had been nominated, all this lost its *raison d'être*. The government which Schleicher had helped to put together was predominantly made up of aristocratic 'gentlemen' of con-servative–nationalist complexion. Thus the East Prussian re-gional administrator (*Landschaftsdirektor*) Freiherr Wilhelm von Gayl had been made Reich Minister of the Interior. There were Lutz Count Schwerin von Krosigk as Finance Minister, Magnus von Braun as Minister of Agriculture and Constantin von Neu-rath as Foreign Minister. The Bavarian DNVP-man Franz Gurt-ner had been nominated Minister of Justice. Collectively they represented a sort of political 'gentlemen's club' whose anti-re-publicanism could be easily gauged by looking at the political career of most of the members of the Papen Cabinet. Talking in confidence to the new Minister of Agriculture Hindenburg was relieved to be able to state that the 'time of republican ministers' was now over.[17] The Republic was ruled by a conservative *fronde* which was determined to do away with the last remnants of Social Democratic and unionist influence which Brüning had still taken account of. They also earnestly believed that in estab-lishing their arch-conservative and authoritarian regime, they would have the support of the Nazis. That they misjudged the situation so badly, demonstrated how underdeveloped were the leadership capacities of the conservative elites who were re-sponsible for the formation of the Papen Cabinet.

This verdict also applies to Schleicher. He thought that, with a political light-weight and former comrade-in-arms as Chancel-lor, he would be able to exert his own influence inside the government all the more effectively. He had also succeeded in placing trusted men, like Erwin Planck, the new State Secretary in the Chancellery, at Papen's side. However, only a few weeks later Schleicher was pained to discover that 'little Franz' (*Fränzchen*) began to show his independence. Through his frivol-ous charm and his unemcumbered panache he quickly gained Hindenburg's favour. Soon he no longer needed Schleicher as his mentor.

17. Thus Otto Braun, quoted in E. Eyck, op.cit., p. 488.

The new Cabinet did not take long to fulfill Hitler's demand for fresh elections. The Reichstag was dissolved on 4 June. It was the beginning of a disastrous policy of advance concessions to the Nazis. But Hitler would not allow himself to be tied down by these concessions. At the beginning of June Schleicher and Papen tried unsuccessfully to forge a coaliton of DNVP, Centre Party and NSDAP. Both politicians also failed to obtain a more long-term Nazi support of the Reich government in return for the lifting of the SA ban. Instead they quickly gave in to a number of ultimata which were accompanied by open threats appearing in Goebbels's papers. Papen, Gayl and Schleicher rescinded the ban with effect from 18 June without having been given any assurances by Hitler. Polling day was fixed for 31 July 1932 and the Nazi movement was now able to demonstrate its power unrestrained and to throw the SA which had meanwhile grown to 400,000 men into the campaign. Meanwhile the Communist paramilitary league remained outlawed. The KPD leader Thälman therefore had a point when he said that the streets had now been cleared for the Nazis to engage in the murber of Communists. But the latter, deeply embittered as they were, pulled no punches on the Nazis as the country plunged into an election campaign waged in a civil-war-type atmosphere. Violence was countered by violence. These bloody battles cost almost one hundred lives up to polling day in Prussia alone. Thousands were injured with the number of victims being roughly the same on either side.

Wilhelm von Gayl, the new Reich Minister of the Interior, sharply condemned the Prussian police for controlling the activities of the SA after the lifting of the ban all too strictly. At a Cabinet meeting on 11 July he bluntly declared that Prussian measures against the Communists were insufficient, adding that the surveillance of the Nazis was wrong and undesirable. From the start, the new Reich government pursued the goal of ousting the Prussian government. At the beginning of July Papen returned, not entirely empty handed, from the negotiations at Lausanne. Thenceforth he had more time to turn his attention to domestic politics and soon the 'Prussian Question' was at the centre of Cabinet activity. The aim was to replace the Braun government by a Reich Commissar and much of the Reich ministers' time was devoted to finding a semi-plausible conditional justification which could be presented to the public. For several weeks, Count Helldorf, the Berlin SA leader, had reported to the *Reichswehr* Ministry his rather imaginary 'anxieties' concerning a common front between the KPD and the *Reichsbanner*. But these arguments were hardly sufficient. Severing, the Prussian Minister of the Interior, had moreover issued another police decree which was designed to demonstrate prophylactically that the Prussian government was not only prepared, but also capable, of intervening even-handedly against left-wing as well as right-wing violence during the election campaign. It was only after an informer in the Police Department of Severing's Ministry had provided fresh information to Gayl that things began to move more quickly. He told Gayl that State Secretary Abegg had received a delegation of leading KPD deputies and had advised them to build up joint defences with the Social Democrats instead of engaging single-handedly in violence against the Nazis. After this, the Reich government thought that they possessed enough 'ammunition' for the intended move against the Prussian government. When the 'preposterous' news was put to Hindenburg, he agreed to sign a decree 'Concerning the Re-establishment of Law and Order in the Territories of the State of Prussia'. Papen and Gayl visited him for this purpose at *Neudeck* in the middle of July. The Reich President also approved the proclamation of the state of siege in Berlin and the surrounding province of Brandenburg to provide a military back-up for the operation.[18]

On 17 July there occurred in Hamburg-Altona the bloodiest street fights waged hitherto between the Nazis and the Communists. Three days later Papen launched his coup against the Prussian government. Papen asked Severing and Heinrich Hirtsiefer, the Prussian Minister for Welfare, who was standing in for Braun, to come to his office. He informed them that they had been dismissed. He added that he had been made Reich Commissar for Prussia. Franz Bracht, the Lord Mayor of Essen, had been nominated Reich Commissar in charge of the Prussian Ministry of the Interior. It was quite obvious that the Constitution had been flagrantly violated. Severing replied that he would give in only if force were applied against him. Later two

18. T. Vogelsang, op.cit., p. 240.

police officers 'occupied' his office, and faced with 'force' in the shape of these two men, he complied without further resistance. And so did the top leadership of the Berlin police presidium following its temporary arrest on the same day.

The events in the police presidium were later recorded by Grzesinski.[19] According to him, he was telephoned by Lieutenant General Gerd von Rundstedt and told that a state of siege had been proclaimed for Berlin and the province of Brandenburg. He also informed Grzesinski that he had been deposed and that Dr Melcher, the Essen police president, had been appointed as his successor. Grzesinski asked for written evidence and added that he wished to consult Severing before he would ring Rundstedt again. But Severing, as Grzesinski quickly learned, was in a defeatist mood and he therefore telephoned Rundstedt again asking him to send Melcher to his office together with the requisite documentation. When Melcher appeared a little later they had an inconclusive conversation, as Grzesinski was still in no mood to budge. After discussions with his advisers, Grzesinski decided that they would vacate their posts only if faced with brute force, and dictated a letter to Rundstedt to this effect. Having received this letter, Rundstedt rang Grzesinski again to express his sympathy, but added that he had no choice but to execute his orders. At 5 p.m. Reichswehr officers and soldiers armed with hand grenades appeared in the presidium. There were further protests and confusion which ended with the arrest of Grzesinski and his deputy half an hour later. As they were led away, their subordinates leaned out of the windows, waving and shouting 'long live the Republic' and 'long live our superiors'. Grzesinski was ushered into a Reichswehr car and driven away. His account concludes: 'I keep on reflecting [on this affair] all the time. For the moment I shan't be entering the police presidium again. Democracy has been dealt a serious blow today in shameful circumstances from which Germany will not recover so quickly'.

No other decision of the Papen government has promoted the later Nazi seizure of power more effectively than the coup against Prussia. The fact that it succeeded virtually without

19. Bundesarchiv Koblenz, Kleine Erwerbungen no. 144, unpubl. notes by Grzesinski of 1933. His description of the July Coup therein is apparently based on a diary he kept on these events.

resistance although Prussia was still thought to be the strongest bastion of the Republic, turned the 20 July 1932 into the *dies ater* of that Republic during its phase of collapse. There were many reasonable grounds for this lack of resistance. To begin with, the Prussian government was a caretaker administration. It had no parliamentary majority and hence lacked full democratic legitimation. Otto Braun, once the strong man of Prussia, was physically and psychically completely exhausted and had withdrawn from his official duties at the beginning of June. The Prussian police had begun to be infiltrated by Nazis at least among its higher-ranking officers. It was no longer as reliable as before and as a force moreover, no match for the *Reichswehr*. The trade union leaders who contemplated calling a general political strike had good reason to doubt if their members would follow a strike call in the face of mass unemployment.

Nevertheless, it is difficult to explain why the Social Democrat leadership in Prussia, the Berlin SPD executive and the *Reichsbanner* headquarters failed to rouse themselves to stage a massive and impressive demonstration. One thing became clear on this fateful day: in the semi-fascist climate which had begun to take hold of the country, the SPD had largely lost confidence in itself. Above all, it had lost the capacity to make an emotionally effective appeal to the masses which tried to capture them beyond the traditional SPD policies of rationality, adherence to legality and *raison d'état*. Political imaginativeness and a will to fight had been progressively stunted in this large republican party and had become replaced by an attentist attitude towards politics. Now, as later during the early months of the Nazi regime, this attention was intended, above all, to wait for, and to survive, the end of this eruption of irrational ideas and aggressions which the SPD found so difficult to comprehend.

The Prussian coup was justified in terms of the alleged need to secure law and order. But its actual calculations emerged in subsequent weeks and months. Almost everywhere in Prussia Social Democrat or left liberal police presidents or regional administrators (*Landräte*) were replaced by conservative civil servants. The bulwark of the Republic was razed to the ground well before the Nazis took over in early February 1933 and under Hermann Göring, Bracht's successor, seized command of the Prussian police and bureaucracy. The ousted government

121

turned to the Prussian Supreme Court (*Staatsgerichtshof*) at Leipzig. Even this body felt bound to concede that the coup had been unconstitutional. But the Court merely ruled that the removal of the Braun government had been unjustified and that the charge that it had failed to demonstrate the required loyalty to the Reich was without foundation. It did not dare to order the restoration of the *status quo ante*. Above all it did not dare to cast doubt on the constitutionality of the decisive presidential decree. Consequently the former ministers of the Braun Cabinet were able to live a shadow existence as the constitutional representatives of Prussia *vis-à-vis* the Diet (which had been reduced to almost complete insignificance) and the *Reichsrat*; but actual power in Prussia lay in the hands of the Reich Commissar who had been appointed in July.

Meanwhile the cause of National Socialism had also begun to flourish in Prussia, as Goebbels cynically noted in his diary only two days after the coup of 20 July 1932: 'A list has been drawn up of the scum [*Kroppzeug*] that will have to be removed in Prussia. A number of newspapers have been banned in various places. Quite a few of us fear that this government might do too much and that nothing will be left for us to do . . . ; the police are remarkably polite. How things have changed in no time.'[20]

For the Reichstag elections of 31 July, the Nazis engaged in a renewed enormous propaganda effort. Hitler's use of an aeroplane on his campaign tours had by now become a routine matter. And yet the Nazi movement barely exceeded the result of the second ballot for the presidential elections three months earlier. This time the Nazis gained 37.8 per cent of the vote and no less than 230 out of 608 seats in the Reichstag. But this was far less than was necessary for a seizure of power based on an absolute parliamentary majority. On the other hand, the NSDAP had now become the largest party in parliament so that Göring was able to assume the office of Reichstag President. Nevertheless, the maximum share which the Nazis succeeded in gaining at the polls during the Weimar Republic had been achieved. There was no further growth in this percentage. The liberal press therefore regarded this result as being a minor blow (*Denkzettel*) for the NSDAP. As to the Nazi leadership, every-

20. J. Goebbels, *Kaiserhof*, p. 133

thing now hinged on the question as to whether its relative passivity towards the Papen Cabinet would pay off and whether Hindenburg and his advisers were in fact prepared to hand the leadership of the government over to Hitler.

However, in view of the vicious campaign which the Nazis had been conducting for the July elections, Papen and Gayl were much less inclined to contemplate such a solution. Above all, Hindenburg refused to drop Papen. As Hitler learned from Schleicher immediately after polling day, the *Führer's* chances of being nominated chancellor were now rather poor. However, the *Reichswehr* minister also gave him the impression that he would continue to advocate a Hitler solution after the Nazi leader had told him that he was absolutely opposed to being given the post of Vice-Chancellor. In order to increase the political pressure, Hitler ordered the SA contingents around Berlin to be reinforced, and during the period immediately following the elections, the SA leaders launched a massive wave of propaganda and demonstrations. Their aim was to make it appear as if a Nazi seizure of power was imminent.

From 6 August Hitler moved to his retreat at Obersalzberg near Berchtesgaden in Upper Bavaria in order to discuss in the circle of the top Nazi leadership what his minimum demands should be. It was agreed that the NSDAP must be given the Reich Chancellorship as well as the posts of Prussian Minister President, Reich Minister of the Interior and Prussian Minister of the Interior. Moreover, the party was to have control of a Reich propaganda Ministry which was to be newly created. Hitler, Strasser, Göring, Frick and Goebbels were singled out as the respective candidates. It was to be the first objective of such a Nazi takeover of the government to obtain approval of a parliamentary Enabling Act which would involve a change of the Constitution. In this way the constant reliance on Hindenburg's presidential powers to issue decrees was to be dispensed with. If the Reichstag rejected such an Enabling bill, the Nazis intended to send the deputies 'home' even if such an action lacked a constitutional basis. As Goebbels put it on 6 August 1932: 'Once we have gained power, we shall never abandon it again, except over our dead bodies.'[21]

21. Ibid., p. 139.

It was a period of tension and highest expectations within the party and the SA. As Goebbels recorded on 8 August: 'The entire party has already geared itself to assuming power. The SA [-men] leave their places of work in order to prepare themselves. The holders of political offices are [likewise] looking towards the great day. . . . The problems relating to a seizure of power are being discussed in detail.'[22]

However, the news which reached Hitler during subsequent days pointed towards a need for scepticism. Under the pressure of continued Nazi acts of violence which had swept through Königsberg and other cities during the previous days, the Cabinet approved a fresh emergency decree on 9 August. It was designed to combat political violence and envisaged the death penalty for political murder. It indicated to Hitler that Papen's preparedness to make concessions was not limitless and was coming to an end. On 10 August, Hindenburg returned to Berlin from his *Neudeck* estate. Papen informed him about Hitler's demands, adding that he would leave the decision entirely to the Reich President. He did not wish to stand in the way. However, Hindenburg vigorously rejected the idea to change the Cabinet. Above all, he was opposed to Hitler becoming Chancellor. For tactical reasons the Nazis had simultaneously begun to explore the possibility of a coalition government with the Centre Party. Such a coalition would have commanded a parliamentary majority. But although he would ultimately have found it very difficult to block the formation of such a coalition, Hindenburg also firmly set his face against this solution. No doubt, the Reich President was satisfied with the arch-conservative Papen government. Moreover, he had meanwhile become used to a situation which, though barely compatible with the Constitution, gave him the decisive prerogative of being able to nominate the government. He did not feel the slightest inclination to take account of the interests of the political parties and of existing parliamentary majorities.

Papen finally sent Hitler who was waiting impatiently an invitation to come to Berlin on 13 August and to have a clarifying discussion with the President. Accompanied by Röhm who was included because Hitler did not wish to risk later criticism

22. Ibid., p. 140.

by the SA, the *Führer* arrived in Berlin and first called on Schleicher. The *Reichswehr* minister told him of Hindenburg's serious qualms. These were further explained to him in a subsequent conversation with Papen. Hitler reproached the Cabinet with great vehemence that measures taken against the 'Marxists' were quite inadequate. The latter were to be 'extinguished root and branch'[23]. This, however, required a strong leadership and a vigour which only he and his movement possessed. Papen retorted that Hitler had promised to support him beyond the Reichstag elections of 31 July. He added that he was prepared to include Nazis in his Cabinet and to use his influence with Hindenburg for the elevation of Hitler to the vice-chancellorship. Hitler bluntly rejected this and could barely be persuaded to meet the Reich President in these circumstances. Hindenburg made the humiliation of the *Führer* complete by asking him with military curtness whether Hitler was prepared to join the present government. When Hitler refused, the President declared without further ado that he found it impossible 'to justify before God, his conscience and the Fatherland the handing-over of all governmental powers to a single party'. Finally he issued a warning to the leader of the Nazi movement. The latter, he said, should conduct his future opposition policies in a 'knightly' manner and to remain 'conscious of his duty to the Fatherland'. He as President would 'counter with all severity' acts of violence of the kind which had regrettably been perpetrated by members of the SA.[24]

Hitler left the Reich President's palace full of rage. He was unavailable even for Schleicher who wanted to mollify him. The President's office issued a press statement later that day through which the 'dressing-down' of Hitler became public knowledge. He had, the statement read bluntly, demanded all power to himself. Hitler and Röhm immediately sent out a joint instruction to the SA leaders ordering them not to start any actions in spite of the rejection by Hindenburg. The *Führer* returned to the Obersalzberg during that same night. He was, it seemed, a defeated man, but he was also thirsting for revenge.

On the following day it became known that during the night five SA men had broken into the home of a Polish worker who

23. T. Vogelsang, op.cit., pp. 263f.
24. Thus Meissner's note on the conversation, repr. in: ibid., pp. 479f.

belonged to the Communists at Potempa in Upper Silesia. Their victim had been trampled to death in the most brutal manner and in front of his mother's eyes. On 22 August a special court at Beuthen imposed the death penalty on the five; this verdict was based on the recent presidential decree. Hitler sent the condemned men an open telegram in which he assured them of his 'unlimited loyalty' in the face of 'this preposterous death sentence'. He also promised them an early release. There followed very sharp attacks in the Nazi press and Papen finally succeeded in persuading Hindenburg to commute the sentences to life imprisonment. Soon after Hitler's seizure of power, in the spring of 1933, the five men were amnestied and released.

The events of 13 August and the Potempa sentence had a traumatic effect on Hitler not dissimilar to the shock he had experienced in Munich during the failed Hitler Putsch at the beginning of November 1923. For a while it seemed as if he was again becoming amenable to the arguments of those of his advisers who had been pressing for some time for putschist action against the 'clique of aristocrats' around Hindenburg and Papen. However, Hitler had not forgotten the lessons from his 1923 Putsch. He knew that, in the final analysis, he would be able to assume power only in alliance with the conservative pillars of the existing state. On the other hand, his telegram to the Potempa murderers had revealed the hatred of the rule of law and the criminal energy seething inside a man who, only a few days previously, had travelled to Berlin to become Reich Chancellor of Germany.

The republican press applauded Hindenburg loudly for his response. What it largely failed to appreciate was that it had been less Hindenburg's adherence to the letter and spirit of the Constitution that had led to Hitler's defeat. Rather he was motivated by his determination to let Papen carry on with his conservative style of government.

The desire to take revenge on Papen was behind a move which the Nazis made on 12 September on the occasion of the opening of the new Reichstag and which was to have unfortunate consequences for the party. Hitler ordered his followers to support a vote of no-confidence against Papen which had been tabled by the Communists. Göring, as Reichstag President, saw to it that a vote was taken. He did so by ignoring a move by

Papen on the government bench to proclaim the dissolution of the Reichstag — a procedure which the Chancellor had prepared to forestall a vote by getting Hindenburg to sign the respective dissolution order. The vote ended with a shattering defeat for Papen. Only 42 deputies supported his Cabinet, with 512 voting against him. There was no more telling proof that the 'cabinet of the barons' lacked completely in political and social support. With the exception of the DVP and DNVP all parties were keen to demonstrate this to Papen and therefore voted for the motion. The dissolution of the Reichstag which the vote of no-confidence had triggered made fresh elections necessary. They were to be held on 6 November. These elections were awkward for Papen. But they were also not in the interests of the Nazis who, following their futile efforts of the spring and summer of 1932 and the all-or-nothing strategy of Hitler, seriously had to reckon with a decline in their electoral support. Working closely with Gayl, Papen was determined after 13 August to end parliamentarism once and for all. At the end of August he had submitted a plan to Hindenburg which envisaged that fresh elections should be postponed for a longer period after the next dissolution of the Reichstag. He accepted that such a postponement might involve a breach of the Constitution. There was a proposal to obtain authority of a long-term prorogation of parliament through a plebiscite. However, given the narrow popular base of the Cabinet, such a move had little chance of success. Hindenburg, who had again retired to *Neudeck* appeared to be prepared to follow Papen's and Gayl's proposals. This is why he had furnished the Chancellor with a prophylactic dissolution order. In the event, Papen had to make use of this order as early as 12 September. As a result the plans to establish an authoritarian regime which had not quite been completed had to be shelved for the time being. For the same reason Hindenburg was also obliged to call fresh elections within the sixty-day limit which the Constitution prescribed.

The track was thus laid for another election on 6 November. It was to cost the Nazis two million of its former voters, but also to usher in the end of the Papen government. The main force behind the fall of Papen was Schleicher. In the middle of November, he formally asked the Chancellor to resign after the latter had failed once again to persuade the NSDAP to support his Cabinet. In the meantime, the general had increasingly come to regard as a major problem the lack of popular support for the government. He was also worried by the almost complete neglect which the Papen government had shown for the trade unions. Finally there was the arbitrary favour extended by an emergency decree of 4 September to industry and agriculture. Schleicher was afraid that the *Reichswehr* might get involved in a civil war-like situation against both the Nazis and the socialist working-class movement, if a stabilisation of Papen's authoritarian government was attempted on this narrow basis by resorting to a breach of the Constitution.

In presenting these worries to Hindenburg, Schleicher succeeded at the beginning of December 1932 in persuading the Reich President to dismiss Papen and to nominate the general Chancellor. This decision followed the renewed failure of Hitler to gain, in talks and negotiations lasting from 19–21 November, the President's confidence as the potential leader of a presidential cabinet. At the same time Schleicher also conducted his own discussions with a number of Nazis who he hoped would be prepared to join a Cabinet under his leadership. Schleicher therefore took a more political approach to the renewed government crisis than did Papen whose conservative–authoritarian plans to commit a breach of the Constitution were barely concealed. His government statement of 15 December made clear that he intended to back away from many of the arbitrary social policies of the reactionary Papen Cabinet. In one sense he might be said to have been willing to trace his steps back halfway to Brüning. However, he was hardly less frivolous in engineering Papen's fall than he had operated during Brüning's demise. Against all expectations, Hitler was to profit from Schleicher's manoeuvres very quickly.

4
The Final Stages of Hitler's Rise to the Chancellorship

4.1. *The Meeting of 4 January 1933*

According to press reports, Hitler was on his way to Detmold on 4 January 1933 to open the campaign for the elections in the tiny state of Lippe-Detmold. Election day was on 15 January, and the entire top brass of the Nazi movement had been mobilised in order to demonstrate that the party had come out of its November depression and was about to surpass its earlier victories. The NSDAP had indeed experienced many trials and tribulations recently. After the great successes of the summer of 1932 it had lost some 15 per cent of its voters mainly to the DNVP and KPD. The local elections in Thuringia on 4 December 1932 had resulted in losses which were in some cases catastrophic. Membership cards were being returned; intra-party criticism was mounting and party finances were in a parlous state. These developments merely exacerbated the mounting tensions inside th Nazi movement. Further setbacks followed. First there was the renewed refusal of Hindenburg to consider Hitler as Papen's successor. Hitler's stubbornnes in demanding the chancellorship for himself had also resulted in the breakdown of the talks with Papen's eventual successor, Kurt von Schleicher. Worse was to come: Gregor Strasser, the NSDAP's second man and its best organiser who was the member of the top leadership to have the highest reputation among the parties of the middle and moderate Right and whom they saw as the main potential coalition partner, had a bitter disagreement with Hitler over the latter's uncompromising stance. On 8 December Strasser resigned from all his positions in the party unleashing a wave of great anxiety, particularly among the regional and local party leaders and among the Nazi deputies in the Reichstag.

Given the depressed state in which the NSDAP found itself at the beginning of the New Year, few people noticed that Hitler stopped over in Cologne on his way to Detmold. Arriving at Cologne at 11 a.m. Hitler got into a rented car and, camouflaged in this way, drove to the residence of Kurt Freiherr von Schröder, a banker, who lived in the affluent *Stadtwaldgürtel* district of the city. Having made his way from Düsseldorf thirty miles further north, Papen arrived at about the same time. Neither of the two men noticed that a newspaper photographer, who had taken up position nearby, took a photo of their arrival.

Among the small group of Hitler's advisers was Wilhelm Keppler, the owner of a small factory producing gelatine. Keppler was an NSDAP member of long standing. Acting as one of the *Führer*'s advisers on economic affairs he had been active during the past ten months establishing contacts with industry through his Keppler Circle. Keppler and Schröder had arranged the meeting between Hitler and Papen after the ex-Chancellor had given a lecture before the Berlin *Herrenklub* just before Christmas. The Cologne banker, a sympathiser and patron of the NSDAP, had acted as a particularly active mediator for his Nazi friends before. In the middle of November 1932, he and Schacht above all had initiated a submission to the Reich President which had been signed by fifteen industrialists. They had asked though without success, that following Papen's dismissal the new Cabinet should contain members of the Nazi movement in leading positions. Apart from Schacht, there were now a number of prominent representatives of heavy industry in the Ruhr, among them Fritz Thyssen, Paul Reusch and Albert Vogler, as well as some other influential bankers and business-men who, like Schröder, belonged to a growing minority in big business. This minority advised that, in order to stabilise the presidential regime and to put the economy back on an even keel, the leadership in the Cabinet should be left to the Nazis. They had been driven to this position all the more strongly when the Communists emerged much strengthened from the November elections. Their fear was that a further crumbling of Nazi support would benefit the KPD. There was also the fact that Schleicher, in his radio address of 15 December in which he presented his government's programme, had, in contradistinc-tion to Papen, presented himself as a 'socially-minded general' and had advocated a broadening of the government base not just towards the Right. Rather he spoke of an inclusion of the Left reaching as far as the Christian and Social Democratic trade unions. This posture had been received with a sigh of relief among the forces of the democratic Left and Centre. But it had been noted with considerable disquiet within the ranks of the conservative Right. This was therefore one of the reasons why Schleicher quickly lost the backing of heavy industry and agriculture which Papen had enjoyed during his chancellorship.

The discussion at the Schröders began with an attempt to deal with the legacy of past conflicts. After the traumatic events of 13 August and the conviction of the Potempa murderers on 22 August, the Nazis had trained their heavy artillery on Papen for several months. Feigning his unabated anger, Hitler came back to these events while Papen tried to mollify him. Not he, the ex-Chancellor protested, but Schleicher had had a hand in the events of 13 August. In order to gain Hitler's full confidence, he then informed him of Schleicher's intrigues in connection with his own dismissal on 1–2 December. He also told him how annoyed Hindenburg had been by Schleicher's behaviour.

Subsequently, even the *Völkischer Beobachter* hinted that in the course of the talks on 4 January 'Herr von Papen' had 'felt the urge' to provide 'the leader of the strongest party [with] certain interesting details concerning the prehistory of his downfall'.[1] He had also told him of 'the methods with which it is possible to become Chancellor these days'. It is not less significant that, when the Cologne meeting was prepared, Hitler had learned via Keppler that Schleicher was *persona non grata* with the Reich President because of his role in the fall of Papen. This was a crucial point which Papen reinforced on 4 January. The rest of the Papen–Hitler talks proceeded almost automatically from there. Papen indicated that it was by no means out of the question that Hitler might be given a leading position in the government if he — Papen — exerted his still considerable influence with Hindenburg and if the two of them combined in a kind of duumvirate.

The discussions, later corroborated, though not without contradictions, by statements and the memoirs of the participants, appear to have moved along these or similar lines. Probably

---

1. *Völkischer Beobachter (Süddeutsche Ausgabe)*, 7./8.1.1933.

Hitler also repeated what he had assured the Reich President in November: he did not wish to gain total power. All he desired was the chancellorship. He was quite agreeable to Hindenburg appointing a foreign minister and a *Reichswehr* minister of his own choice. Nor was he averse to taking over the conservative 'expert' ministers serving in the existing government.

Hitler and Papen left the Schröder residence at about 3 p.m. after agreeing to continue the talks. They thought that it would be possible to keep their renewed contact secret. However, on the following day the Berlin *Tägliche Rundschau*, which was close to Schleicher, carried the news of the meeting in big letters and included the photographic evidence. The item had the effect of a bomb explosion. Papen, Hitler and Schröder were forced to play down the meeting in public. The press began to speculate as to whether this was an intrigue by Papen against Schleicher, his former protector and friend. Or was it no more than a non-committal exchange of views?

Pretty much at the same time when the Hitler–Papen meeting was adjourned in the afternoon of 4 January 1933, Hindenburg received Gregor Strasser. The audience had been recommended to the Reich President by the Chancellor. The latter had still not abandoned his plan to gain, with Strasser's help, the support of parts of the NSDAP for his government. This hope persisted, notwithstanding the fact that Strasser had retreated to South Tyrol after his break with Hitler. Nor had Strasser done anything to foster an active opposition movement within the party so that Hitler was given ample opportunity of more or less reconsolidating the party's position by means of a quick redistribution of Strasser's powers as head of the NSDAP's national organisation (*Reichsorganisationsleiter*). When Strasser had left, Hindenburg is reported to have said: 'This man is cutting a very different figure than this Hitler. I like Strasser much better.' The President was in principle also quite happy with Strasser's appointment to the vice-chancellorship which Schleicher had envisaged. But the Chancellor did not press his case. He had come to realise that such a move could no longer have the same effect which it would have at the end of November or in early December. At that point he had told Hindenburg that, unlike Papen, he would be able to engineer, with Strasser's help, a participation of the Nazis in the Cabinet which did not included Hitler.

Based largely on this argument, he had strongly advised the reich President against Papen's plan to send the Reichstag 'home' for a longer period and to appoint an emergency government thereby breaching the Constitution. Schleicher warned that this solution to the crisis would result in a civil-war-like escalation of the ruthless opposition of Nazis and Communists against the Papen Cabinet which was supported by no more than a small minority of conservatives. When on 1 December Hindenburg nevertheless decided to hold on to Papen to whom he had developed a certain attachment, Schleicher laid the results of a *Reichswehr* staff exercise before him. This document contained a very pessimistic prognosis of the future, if the Papen Cabinet were allowed to continue. Faced with this evidence Hindenburg had very reluctantly agreed to Papen's dismissal and Schleicher's nomination as Chancellor on 2 December. This has been the 'intrigue' which Papen refused to forgive his successor.

Hitler's refusal to co-operate with the Schleicher Cabinet and the resigned attitude of Strasser following his break with Hitler had led to a deterioration of Schleicher's position very soon after his assumption of power. This deterioration was a major prerequisite of the Papen–Hitler *rapprochement*. Above all, Schleicher had failed to prevent Hindenburg from including his erstwhile favourite chancellor in his circle of advisers. The ephemeral character of Schleicher's chancellorship was symbolised by the fact that Papen continued to live in the official Reich Chancellor's residence directly adjacent to the Reich President's place. Schleicher meanwhile continued to work from his old office at the *Reichswehr* Ministry which was situated in the *Bendlerstrasse*.

After Schleicher had obtained incontrovertible proof of the secret meeting between Hitler and Papen, he lodged a complaint about his predecessor with Hindenburg. He asked 'the old gentleman' only to conduct conversations with Papen in future if he, the Chancellor, was present. However, the 85-year-old President had become used since the days of Brüning to talk with unofficial advisers about the fate of a particular chancellor behind the latter's back. Of course, for a long time it had been Schleicher, above all, who had exploited to the full this opportunity of wielding influence behind the scenes. Even if Hindenburg had had a better appreciation of the meaning of loyalty, he was unlikely to be convinced by these reproaches against Papen coming, as they did, from Schleicher's mouth. It was only on 9 January that Papen paid the Chancellor a visit to inform him of his meeting with Hitler. He then immediately, and without Schleicher, proceeded to the President's palace. He gave Hindenburg a much more detailed report. Schleicher's complaints notwithstanding, Papen learned 'with satisfaction that the old gentleman had no criticism to make of the new activities of his old Chancellor'.[2] Otto Meissner, Hindenburg's State Secretary, later gave the following description of the meeting:

> No other person was present on 9 January when Papen reported to Reich President von Hindenburg about the attitude which Hitler had displayed at the Cologne meeting. However, the President [later] informed me that Hitler, in the course of this discussion with Papen, had backed away from his earlier demand that he should be given total power and would now be prepared in principle to participate in a coalition government. He, Hindenburg, had agreed that Papen should personally and on his basis keep in touch with Hitler; since Hitler was not prepared to support or tolerate the present Schleicher government, a new cabinet was the only alternative whose head he envisaged Papen to be.[3]

Papen has time and again after 1945 tried to give the impression that his talks with Hitler at Cologne had not been directed against Schleicher. Nor allegedly did they serve to produce a counter-government containing Hitler and Papen. Meissner's memoirs and a number of other sources clearly contradict this view. Above all, there is Goebbels's diary in which he recorded on 6 January in connection with 'Hitler's talks in Cologne':[4] 'Papen wants to topple Schleicher.' Other works have frequently quoted the version which Goebbels published in 1934 in his *Vom Kaiserhof zur Reichskanzlei*: 'If this coup succeeds, we shan't be too distant for [gaining] power.' However, since the discovery of the original diary, this latter sentence is now known to be a retrospective stylisation.

2. See A. Dorpalen, *Hindenburg in der Geschichte der Weimarer Republik*, Berlin 1966, p. 389.
3. O. Meissner, *Staatssekretär unter Ebert — Hindenburg — Hitler*, Hamburg 1950, pp. 261f.
4. See chap. 1, note 2, above.

4.2. *The Mobilisation of the Reichslandbund*

Among the lobbyists who moved around the 'court' of the Reich President, Hindenburg's noble peers and estate-owning friends had long been particularly successful. It was thanks to these friends that the Hindenburg had been given back as a gift the Neudeck family estate in the East Prussian Rosenberg district which had been irredeemably lost because of over-indebtedness. On the initiative of Elard von Oldenburg-Januschau, Hindenburg's East Prussian neighbour and political adviser, a committee had been constituted soon after Hindenburg had been elected President in 1925. Largely through donations from industry it became possible to purchase the estate and to put it back into viability with the help of the state-funded *Osthilfe*, an aid programme to support Prussia's ailing landowners. Neudeck was officially given to Hindenburg on the occasion of his eightieth birthday in 1927. In order to keep it in the family and to avoid death duty, the son and adjutant of the old Field Marshal, Colonel Oskar von Hindenburg, had been registered as the legal owner of the land-title.

The *Osthilfe* aid for Neudeck became the subject of renewed discussion in the Berlin press at the beginning of January. This discussion had been triggered by an article by Erich Ludendorff, Hindenburg's arch-enemy.[5] The topic became even more explosive when on 10 January Social Democratic and Centre Party members of the Reichstag Budget Committee began to scrutinise the use of *Osthilfe* funds by East Elbian landowners. Various serious frauds had already come to light. The allegations included charges that the funds had been used to pay for gambling debts, the acquisition of race horses, for holiday trips to the Riviera and the keeping of mistresses. Members of the oldest noble families appeared to be involved in the scandal. There was even a rumour that 'relatives of the Reich President had profited from the irregularities'.[6]

These developments were accompanied by massive attacks by the *Reichslandbund* (RLB) and its regional organisations against the Schleicher Cabinet. On 6 January, Goebbels's *Angriff* had published no less than eighteen protest letters submitted by

5. *Vossische Zeitung*, 4.1.1933.
6. See A. Dorpalen, op.cit., p. 392.

agrarian associations to the government. Moreover, in December 1931 Werner Willikens, one of the leading men in the agrarian organisation of the NSDAP, had been made one of the four RLB presidents. During the 1932 election campaigns the Nazis had also succeeded in gaining a foothold in the agrarian associations of the Protestant north and east. These shifts increasingly coloured the style of RLB agitation against the Schleicher government. At the instigation of the Nazis, the Pomeranian Chamber of Agriculture, in a letter dated 6 January 1933, even went so far as to reproach the Reich Chancellor that he was behind a campaign of vilification by the 'anti-agrarian Jewish press in Berlin' against the agricultural policies which 'the Herr Reich President had approved'.[7] On 15 December 1932, in his government statement, Schleicher had hinted that he would prove a bit more resistant to agrarian lobbyism than his predecessor Papen. He also used the occasion to reopen the question of agricultural resettlement in the East which was embarrassing for the estate-owners. These moves were sufficient for the agrarian interest groups to suspect Schleicher, as they had done in the case of Brüning, of being an 'agrarian Bolshevik'. As the *Frankfurter Zeitung* put it on 12 January 1933: 'Pampered by the generosity with which Herr von Papen helped agriculture', it had not taken more than a few mild indications of 'increased resistance' on the part of the Reich Chancellor for the RLB to resort to shameful threats. The paper referred to a resolution by the RLB presidium of 11 January which attacked, in demagogic fashion, 'the pillaging of agriculture in favour of the almighty pecuniary interests of the internationally-minded export industries and its satellites'. The presidium asserted that the impoverishment of agriculture, 'tolerated by the present government as it is', had assumed proportions 'which were not even deemed possible under a Marxist government'.[8]

In the morning of that day the RLB leadership had been received by Hindenburg. The audience had probably been arranged by Oskar von Hindenburg, as State Secretary Meissner was on holiday at this time. The RLB leaders put their demands and sharply criticised the Schleicher Cabinet. The six-man del-

---

7. Quoted in H. Gies, R. *Walther Darré und die nationalsozialistische Bauernpolitik in den Jahren 1930 bis 1933*, Coblenz 1966, p. 127.
8. See *Frankfurter Zeitung*, 12.1.1933.

egation was headed by the executive president, Eberhard Count von Kalckreuth, who had played a leading role in Brüning's fall in May 1932 and who, in November 1932, had signed the open letter to Hindenburg which prominent industrialists had initiated, urging the Reich President to take the Nazis into the government. The delegation also included Willikens, the Nazi member in the RLB presidium.

Schleicher was most put off that Hindenburg first received the delegation on its own. The Chancellor and his Ministers of Agriculture and Economics were asked to join them only in the second half. It was even more embarrassing to see how Hindenburg digressed from the main issue on the agenda, i.e. the demand of the RLB to protect estates against the receiver if mortgage facilities were withdrawn. The President rejected the Chancellor's point in the presence of the RLB leaders, demanded in what sounded almost like a military command 'that the Cabinet be convened this evening to ratify the bills as desired [by the President] and to submit them to me for signature tomorrow morning'.[9] The abovementioned RLB resolution was made public only after the meeting. Schleicher reacted furiously. 'This resolution', he informed the press, 'was not given to either the Reich President or the Reich government before the meeting. Had this been the case, the Herr Reich President would have cancelled the reception of the *Reichslandbund*.' The government, at any rate, would refuse 'to enter into negotiations with members of the *Reichslandbund* executives forthwith'.[10]

The dissension between the government and the agrarians was welcome to, above all, the Nazis. As Goebbels noted in his diary:[11] 'This suits us nicely at the moment.' But it also suited Papen in his endeavours to include Hugenberg's DNVP in a new government to be formed in collaboration with Hitler. The Nationalists were in basic agreement with the demands of the agrarians. But since the days of the Harzburg Front meeting in October 1931 their relationship with the NSDAP had become increasingly precarious and competitive.

Schleicher met Hugenberg three days after the conflict with

9. See A. Dorpalen, op.cit., p. 391.
10. See *Frankfurter Zeitung*, 12.1.1933.
11. J. Goebbels, *Kaiserhof*, p. 241.

the RLB. He wanted to find out under what conditions the DNVP might be prepared to enter his Cabinet. Hugenberg insisted that he should be given both the Ministry of Agriculture and the Ministry of Economics. Schleicher indicated that this was not acceptable to him, if only out of regard for the Centre Party and the trade unions who, he hoped, he could win over to 'tolerate' his government.[12]

4.3. *Hectic Activity at Ribbentrop's House*

For the last six months, Hitler had gained another intermediary with Papen in Berlin. This was Joachim von Ribbentrop, an importer with overseas experience, who had been to Turkey on a military mission with Papen during the First World War and who had since kept in touch with him. Ribbentrop's weekend cottage in the Berlin suburb of Dahlem was to become the focus of hectic political negotiations. According to Ribbentrop's notes, Papen and Hitler met again at his cottage on the night of 10–11 January, less than a week after their Cologne encounter. After this came polling day in Lippe-Detmold on 15 January when the Nazis succeeded in recovering some of the voters lost on 6 November 1932, but failed to reach the level of support achieved on 31 July. This was a success which helped to strengthen Hitler's self-confidence. It looked as if the Strasser crisis had been overcome. Hitler returned to Berlin on the evening of 17 January to hold a meeting with Hugenberg later that night. But the atmosphere between the DNVP leader and him remained frosty. A further meeting between Papen and the '*Führer*' took place on the following day at Ribbentrop's cottage in the presence of Göring, Röhm and Himmler, the leader of the SS. According to Ribbentrop's records: 'Hitler insisted on [being given the] chancellorship; Papen again thinks this impossible. It went beyond his influence with Hindenburg to get this accepted.'[13]

On 20 January the Reichstag's Council of Elders resolved that the next session was to begin on 31 January. This date provided a clearer timescale for the calculations of the divergent political

---

12. See F. von Papen, *Der Wahrheit eine Gasse*, Munich 1952, p. 262.
13. J. von Ribbentrop, *Zwischen London und Moskau*, Leoni 1953, p. 39.

focus and accelerated the decision-making process. It was generally assumed that this Reichstag meeting would culminate in a no-confidence motion against the Schleicher Cabinet, following Schleicher's failure to broaden its basis of political support. On 31 January at the latest it would become clear whether the Chancellor had the Reich President's authority to dissolve parliament and to announce fresh elections or whether he had even been given powers to form an unconstitutional emergency cabinet and to send the Reichstag 'home' for a longer period.

In the face of the hectic activity in the Papen–Hitler camp, Schleicher displayed an 'Olympic calm', as the *Frankfurter Zeitung* put it on 23 January. This stance was commented upon by the pro-Schleicher press in a tone of growing irritation. Papen had resumed contact with Hindenburg on 19–20 January. For the first time he now promoted the idea of handing the Chancellorship to Hitler, arguing that sufficient safeguards could be built in against a one-party dictatorship by the Nazis. In putting forward this proposal, Papen quickly found that Hindenburg's instinctive aversion against Hitler was undiminished. In particular Oskar von Hindenburg backed up his father on this point. Oskar's qualms were based not so much on political insight than on an arrogant sense of superiority *vis-à-vis* the demagogic upstart Hitler which was widespread among the nobility and the officer corps. This is why Papen first tried to change Oskar's mind by arranging a personal encounter between him and the Nazi leader. The President agreed, and Oskar insisted for his part that State Secretary Meissner should accompany him to the meeting which had been arranged at Ribbentrop's for 22 January.

All participants were trying hard to keep this meeting secret. Oskar von Hindenburg and Meissner first went to an opera performance together. During the intermission they circulated among the other visitors in the foyer. But shortly after the beginning of the last act they quietly left their box and took a taxi to Dahlem. Meanwhile Hitler had made a public appearance at an SA rally in the Berlin *Sportpalast* to commemorate the third anniversary of the death of Horst Wessel. After this meeting he proceeded to Ribbentrop's cottage together with Göring. Papen reached the meeting-place after he had been to a rally of the *Stahlhelm* ex-Servicemen's Association.

For the following two hours Hitler talked to Oskar von Hindenburg on his own. His arguments were the old ones: he alone would be able to rescue Germany from the threat of Communism. No government would be able to survive without his support. Were he to become Chancellor, he would strictly observe the prerogatives of the Reich President under Article 48 and his supreme command of the armed forces. He would also adhere to the constitution. Supported by his own party which commanded one third of the Reichstag seats and by other 'patriotic' forces on the Right and in the Centre, he, through the passage of a parliamentary enabling act, would be able to achieve a constitutional prorogation of the Reichstag, etc. etc. However, it appears that Hitler blended such arguments, which were designed to win Oskar von Hindenburg over to his side, with open threats: if, he added, he were not made Chancellor, a criminal investigation might have to be reckoned with against the President concerning his role in the *Osthilfe* transactions.

As Oskar confessed to Meissner on their way home, he was very impressed by Hitler's arguments and had now himself gained the conviction that Hitler should be given the post of Chancellor. However, at first he merely succeeded in weakening the resistance of his father to this idea, but failed to remove the President's qualms altogether, as Papen was to learn when he met the old Field Marshal for another conversation on the following morning. At this point Schleicher inadvertently helped his opponent Papen to overcome the deadlock. The Chancellor had learned of the meeting between Oskar and Hitler through his own *Reichswehr* intelligence network. Highly alarmed by this news, he asked for an audience with Hindenburg on the morning of 23 January. The meeting ended rather disastrously for Schleicher.

To begin with, he had to admit to Hindenburg that his attempts to obtain the support of the Nazis and other political forces for a stabilisation of his government had failed and that he might have to face a vote of no-confidence in the Reichstag on 31 January. Schleicher now proposed that parliament should be dissolved and that fresh elections be postponed beyond the sixty-day period prescribed by the Constitution by invoking an emergency. Hindenburg now reminded Schleicher that he had opposed this solution only two months ago when the then

Chancellor Papen submitted it to him and that he had done so by reference to the threat of a civil war which would put the *Reichswehr* into an awkward position. Schleicher tried to explain that the situation was now much more favourable than eight weeks earlier. He could count on trade union passivity. Moreover, this time he combined the political and the military power in his own hands. Hindenburg refused to accept this reasoning. The President replied: 'He would think about the question of a dissolution of the Reichstag;' however he would find it impossible 'at the present moment [!] to take responsibility for a postponement of the elections beyond the date laid down in the Constitution'. Such a move would be interpreted 'by all sides as a breach of the Constitution' on his part.[14]

The minutes of the meeting clearly demonstrate one thing: Hindenburg was not willing to concede to Schleicher what he had been prepared to grant Papen two months earlier. It is noticeable how much he stressed his concern over a breach of the Constitution, and it is possible that these worries had grown since the problem of his role in the *Osthilfe* scandal had begun to loom larger. More probably, however, his constitutional qualms were merely a pretext. After all, the encounter confirmed that, although Hindenburg was still opposed to Hitler's chancellorship, he expected quite firmly that Papen would succeed in his moves to offer an alternative to the Schleicher Cabinet. No doubt he was also hoping that Papen would be able to 'incorporate' the Nazis and thus create the preconditions of the passage of an enabling bill by which the Reichstag voted for its own prorogation. However, Papen had already made clear that such a result could not be achieved without Hitler's nomination as Chancellor. Consequently, the tracks were practically laid in the direction of this outcome, even if Hindenburg took a few days to get used to the idea of a Hitler Cabinet.

Hindenburg indicated in his talks with Schleicher on 23 January and in a subsequent discussion with Hammerstein-Equord, the chief of the *Heeresleitung*, that he continued to be unwilling to give the chancellorship to Hitler. In the confusion of intrigue and counter-intrigue of the following days, the Chancellor and his confidants in the *Reichswehr* Ministry therefore started from

14. Meissner's notes on the conversations between Hindenburg and Schleicher on 23 and 28 January. Copy in the archive of the *Institut für Zeitgeschichte* in Munich.

the erroneous assumption that Papen was still trying to form a new cabinet led by himself, and this they thought was the worst of all possible solutions. Above all, Schleicher and Hammerstein did not know that, in further talks between Hitler, Papen and Hindenburg, a new *Reichswehr* Minister had meanwhile been found. This was General Werner von Blomberg, the commander of the East Prussian military district, who had come to hold very positive views of the NSDAP and also of the auxiliary military role of the SA in the context of the border protection measures in the east against Poland. Blomberg had moreover spoken up against an emergency dictatorship by the President, fearing that this would lead to a confrontation between the *Reichswehr* and the Hitler movement. This stance made him an ideal successor to Schleicher in the eyes of both Hindenburg and Hitler.

4.4. *The Removal of Last-Minute Qualms*

Papen was particularly keen to include in the proposed new government both the DNVP and the *Stahlhelm* ex-Servicemen's Association which had several hundred thousand members and was close to Hindenburg. His hope was that this would make the planned containment of Hitler by conservative ministers to look very convincing and thus remove Hindenburg's objections. When Papen held talks to this effect with the two *Stahlhelm* leaders, Franz Seldte and Theodor Duesterberg, the latter proved intractable. However, Papen obtained the consent of Seldte, an opportunist who was to become Hitler's Minister of Labour. Remembering his many painful disappointments with Hitler, Hugenberg, the DNVP leader, was even more negative than Duesterberg. Not only did he make the same demand as he had put to Schleicher, i.e. that he be given dictatorial powers over the economy through a combination of the ministries of economics and of agriculture in both Prussia and the Reich; he also categorically opposed the idea of handling the post of Prussian Reich Commissar to the Nazis and thereby giving them control of the Prussian police. Finally, on 27 January, Hitler held personal talks with Hugenberg. The conversation ended in acrimony. As Ribbentrop recorded it, the meeting broke up in a huff 'because of the impossible demands of the Nationalists'.

Hitler, who thought once more that all plans had collapsed, wanted to leave for Munich without delay. Again he was seized by the old trauma that he was to be conned into a solution which was unacceptable to him. He was correct in the sense that Papen was secretly also negotiating about a new government, which would be composed exclusively of conservative, non-Nazi ministers. Göring had great trouble persuading the *Führer* to stay in Berlin. In the end he succeeded and it proved worthwhile: the decisive turn of events occurred on the following day.

As Ribbentrop had written in the evening on 27 January:[15] 'Papen now has no doubt whatsoever that he must push through Hitler's chancellorship at all costs and that he cannot go on believing that in any case he must keep himself at Hindenburg's disposal.' In fact, when Papen met the President on the morning of 28 January, he told him in more unambiguous terms than ever before that the success of his solution to the government crisis depended on Hitler being nominated Chancellor. Now the 'softening up' of the President which had occurred in the days prior to 28 January was beginning to bear fruit. Shortly before Papen's arrival the old Field Marshal had been seen by his friend Oldenburg-Januschau. When Hindenburg voiced his qualms about the robust methods of the Nazis, Oldenburg-Januschau calmed him down by remarking jovially that one would know how to deal with those 'young chaps who are basically quite nice'.[16] It may also have had a reassuring effect on Hindenburg that Göring had played an increasingly prominent part in the negotiations. Göring was a highly decorated fighter pilot of the First World War, and he and Frick were to be the only two Nazis in a proposed Hitler Cabinet surrounded by a majority of conservative ministers. In his conversation on 28 January Papen for the first time gained the impression that the President was now prepared to accept Hitler's chancellorship.

At Schleicher's urgent request, Hindenburg received the sitting Chancellor, who had just held a meeting of his Cabinet, immediately after his discussion with Papen. Schleicher had told his Cabinet colleagues that he did not expect to be given presidential authority to dissolve the Reichstag and to send the deputies on an indefinite leave. In view of this, he had obtained

15. J. von Ribbentrop, op.cit., p. 41.
16. See A. Dorpalen, op.cit., p. 407.

their approval that he would announce the resignation of the entire Cabinet, if his assumption proved correct. However, Schleicher had also gained his colleagues' support for his plan to warn Hindenburg explicitly against approving the formation of an ultra-right-wing Papen–Hugenberg government which Schleicher still thought to be in the offing.

According to Meissner's minutes, the meeting between Hindenburg and his Chancellor began a little after midday. Schleicher started off by outlining the different possibilities open to the President to resolve the government crisis: '(1) a majority Cabinet [led by] Hitler; this would be one solution, but he does not think its emergence possible. (2) a minority Cabinet [led by Hitler], but this would not conform to the position which the Reich President had taken up hitherto. (3) retention of the present presidential government provided it had the confidence and the authorisation of the Reich President. Nine-tenths of the German people would be opposed to a government constituted on the narrow basis of the Nationalists etc., but without the National Socialists; this would lead to revolutionary disturbances and to a constitutional crisis (*Staatskrise*). If the present government was to face the Reichstag, he would have to ask to be given a dissolution order. The Reich President replied: 'I cannot do this in the given situation. I gratefully acknowledge that you have tried to win over the National Socialists to your side. This has unfortunately failed, and now the search for other solutions would have to be attempted'.

After this clear rebuke, the minutes merely registered the following appeal by Schleicher: 'When the new Reich government is formed, he asks the Herr Reich President particularly not to nominate a supporter of Hitler for the post of *Reichswehr* Minister. Otherwise the *Reichswehr* would be facing great danger. The Herr Reich President would be facing great danger. The Herr Reich President replied that he absolutely rejected such an idea himself'.[17] Schleicher went away to announce the resignation of his Cabinet. Meanwhile Papen was called to see Hindenburg for a second time. In the course of this meeting, at which his son and Meissner were present, the President finally said it was now his duty to install Hitler as Chancellor. He did so

17. Meissner's notes (see note 14).

with an air of resignation and not without deliberately pointing to the responsibility which his advisers shared in this matter. Then he asked Papen to explore the possibility of forming a Hitler Cabinet 'within the framework of the Constitution' and supported by the relevant parties in the Reichstag. He also stipulated that Papen should take over the post of Vice-Chancellor and of Prussian Reich Commissar. This stipulation confronted Papen with his most difficult task. Laborious negotiations ensued with Göring and Hitler at the end of which Papen agreed to a pseudo-compromise: Göring was to be the Reich Commissar's deputy in charge of the Prussian Ministry of the Interior. On this basis Hugenberg also agreed to join in. It took Hitler and his advisers a lot to swallow Hugenberg's demand that he should be given all government departments concerned with economic affairs. Papen saw Hindenburg again on 29 January to report these results to him. In the afternoon of that day Göring had happy news for Hitler who was staying in Goebbels's flat: the deal had been sown up; Hindenburg was ready to receive Hitler and his future cabinet colleagues at 11 a.m. on 30 January for the swearing-in ceremony.

Later that night Hindenburg and Papen received news of an irritating rumour: Schleicher was said to be wanting to mobilise the *Reichswehr* and to declare a state of siege. Papen now suggested to the President that he should immediately put Blomberg in charge of the *Reichswehr* and before the official constitution of the new Cabinet. Blomberg by this time was on his way back from the disarmament talks at Geneva, and when he arrived early next morning at Anhalter Station he was met there by Oskar von Hindenburg. The other person to meet Blomberg at the station was Hammerstein's adjutant. But the general did not follow the request of his immediate superior, Hammerstein; he accepted the invitation of his ultimate superior, Hindenburg, and went to the Reich President's palace in the company of Oskar. Hinderburg immediately made Blomberg *Reichswehr* Minister and asked him to take the oath.

A few hours later Hitler, Papen and the other nominees for the new Cabinet gathered in Meissner's office. There are four members of the Schleicher Cabinet who were supposed to be included in the new government: Constantin von Neurath, the Foreign Minister, Lutz Count Schwerin von Krosigk as Finance

Minister, Franz Gürtner, the Minister of Justice, and Transport Minister Paul von Eltz-Rübenach.

When reporting back to Hindenburg on the previous day that a consensus had been achieved by all concerned on all essential points, Papen had omitted one important issue: Hugenberg was opposed to Hitler's idea to hold Reichstag elections for one last time in order to provide the new government with an absolute majority. The DNVP leader rightly feared that his party would be knuckled under in the process. At 11.15 a.m. Hitler and Hugenberg could still be seen haggling over this point. They were interrupted by Meissner who asked the two men sternly not to keep the President waiting any longer. Barely uttering a word, Hindenburg administered the oath. Hitler had been made Chancellor. He gave a solemn pledge that he would abide by the Constitution and respect the rights of the President. His words sounded hollow and disappeared in the reception hall without echo.

4.5. *Postscript*

At first glance the intrigues which paved Hitler's way to the Reich Chancellery leave the impression that the collapse of the Weimar Republic was, above all, the result of personal vanities, ambitions and interests, propelling the conservative-nationalist power-elites around Hindenburg. On closer examination we can see that there was, behind these coincidences, a certain logic which, from Brüning's fall onwards, became increasingly inescapable.

When Papen took office and the Social Democrat-led Prussian government was unseated, an irreversible decision had been made to rule through an authoritarian right-wing regime which was not supported by parliament and, in particular, did not take any notice of the political Left, i.e. the SPD and the trade unions. Schleicher made a belated attempt to return to a better balanced system supported by a combination of forces reaching from the Nazis and Nationalists to the unions. But this attempt foundered on the interests and ambitions of industry, large-scale agriculture and other conservative-nationalist forces. These forces had been strengthened by the Papen regime, and they were more determined than they had been during the Brüning period that no attempt should be made to overcome the crisis of Weimar parliamentarianism and its welfare system with the help of a *temporary* application of authoritarian policies. Rather what they envisaged was to exploit the crisis in order to deliberately bring about a permanent change of the Constitution in an authoritarian direction. Some even considered the possibility of a restoration of the monarchy. Article 48 of the Weimar Constitution and the powerful position of the Reich President as a kind of 'substitute monarch' offered constitutional levers to achieve this effect. More importantly, Hindenburg and his advisers had begun to use these presidential prerogatives well beyond the spirit of the Constitution and with the aim of purposeful constitutional change very much in mind. The special role of the *Reichswehr* in this process also pointed to an attempt to revive the military structures of the Prusso-German monarchy. This development had set in under Brüning and was embodied above all by Schleicher and his policy to gain a dominant influence on government formation and government policy through direct army links with the President outside the sphere not only of parliament, but also of Cabinet decision-making.

However, the conservative–nationalist forces that aimed at a restoration of this kind were incapable of providing a popular backing for it. And yet without a plebiscitarian base a stabilisation of the situation which industry and commerce, crisis-stricken as they were, were also calling for more and more impatiently, proved ultimately impossible. In this respect the authoritarian presidential governments of Papen and Schleicher remained dependent on the support of the NSDAP and this, in turn, made them vulnerable to blackmail by the Hitler movement.

Lack of popularity was the reproach which Brüning had to face many times towards the end of his term of office; this weakness decisively weakened the prestige and the power base of his government. The absence of a popular basis condemned the Papen Cabinet even more strikingly to an ephemeral existence. It was no more than a transitional government on the way to a Nazi seizure of power. Hindenburg refused to hand power to Hitler for a long time. But when he finally and at the last minute changed his mind he was also motivated by a desire to restore the popularity of his presidential regime. Schleicher proposed the risky establishment of a military dictatorship; Papen promised to deliver a popular base, and, faced with this choice, Hindenburg opted for the latter solution.

What increased the dependence of the old anti-republican and conservative–nationalist elites on Hitler was that nationalist and *völkische* ideologies had begun to corrode established traditional principles of government and legality well before 1933. The boundaries between Papen's Young Conservatism and the varied elements of the 'Conservative Revolution' that had rallied within the broad framework of Nazism had become fluid long ago.

What provided the glue for the 'fateful' and never harmonious alliance between the conservative elites and the Nazi mass movement which made Hitler's chancellorship possible, was the aggressive rejection of Weimar parliamentarism and of the forces that had shaped the Republic. These latter forces — Social Democrats, left liberals and Centre Party Catholics — had been decried as 'Reich enemies' as early as the Bismarckian Empire. The Weimar Republic, in its more stable days and represented by politicians like Gustav Stresemann, was on its way to bring about the political reconciliation and alliance of Right and Left, i.e. of the conservative or national–liberal bourgeoisie and of the democratic-socialist and Christian-social popular movements. The Nazis addressed the desire of large sections of the population for political and social emancipation, but they did so not in a rational and responsible manner, but by appealing to emotions, aggressions and utopian longings. They thereby made a radical break with the slow evolution towards a more democratic society, which had set in during the late Wilhelmine period and had continued under the Weimar Republic. The Nazis disenfranchised, persecuted and exiled the spokesmen of these democratising currents. They did so in the name of a vague notion of a future state based on the principles of leadership and *Volksgemeinschaft*. No more than a bare half of the population had voted for the establishment of this type of regime in free elections even at the height of the crisis. Mobilising their dreams and their deeply-felt sense of humiliation which, following the Versailles Treaty, had turned these groups against the Weimar Republic as the symbol of the defeat of 1918–19, Hitler embarked upon an experiment in plebiscitarian dictatorship which was at first tremendously successful. These successes, which were carried forward by feelings of elation and by the lure of participating in a social and patriotic *Erhebung* (uprising) misled many Germans into overlooking the manifestations of terror which accompanied the Hitler 'experiment' from the start. The extent to which this indifference to injustice and brutality occurred is nevertheless staggering.

Select Bibliography

This bibliography is designed to provide some further specialised reading on the main aspects covered by this book. It lists only English-language monographs and is divided by themes.

The beginnings of the Nazi movement

Diehl; J.M., *Paramilitary Politics in Weimar Germany*, Bloomington, 1977

Gordon, H.J., *The Reichswehr and the German Republic*, Princeton, 1957

—, *Hitler and the Beer Hall Putsch*, Princeton, 1972

Lane, B.M., and L.J. Rupp. (eds.), *Nazi Ideology before 1933*, Austin, 1978

Merkl, P.H., *Political Violence under the Swastika*, Princeton, 1975

—, *The Making of a Stormtrooper*, Princeton, 1980

Nicholls, A.J., *Weimar and the Rise of Hitler*, London, 1968

Noakes, J., *The Nazi Party in Lower Saxony*, Oxford, 1971

Nyomarkay, J., *Charisma and Factionalism in the Nazi Party*, Minneapolis, 1967

Orlow, D., *The History of the Nazi Party*, 2 vols., Newton Abbot, 1973

Pridham, G., *Hitler's Rise to Power*, London, 1973

Stachura, P.D., *Nazi Youth in the Weimar Republic*, Santa Barbara, 1975

Waite, R.G.L., *Vanguard of Nazism*, Cambridge, Mass., 1952

Biographies of Hitler

Binion, R., *Hitler among the Germans*, New York, 1976

Bullock, A., *Hitler*, New York, 1964

Carr, W., *Hitler*, London, 1978

Fest, J., *Hitler*, London, 1974

Stern, J.P., *Hitler*, London, 1975

Stone, N., *Hitler*, London, 1980

Waite, R.G.L., *The Psychopathic God*, New York, 1977

Select Biography

German Society and Voting Behaviour

Bessel, R., *Political Violence and the Rise of Nazism*, New Haven, 1985
Childers, T., *The Nazi Voter*, Chapel Hill, 1984
Fischer, C., *Stormtroopers*, London, 1983
Hamilton, R.F., *Who Voted for Hitler?*, Princeton, 1982
Kele, M.H., *Nazis and Workers*, Chapel Hill, 1972
Lebovics, H., *Social Conservatism and the Middle Classes in Germany*, Princeton, 1969
Niewyk, D.L., *The Jews in Weimar*, Germany, London, 1980
Rosenhaft, E., *Beating the Fascists?* Cambridge, 1983
Stephenson, J., *Women in Nazi Society*, London, 1975

The Economic Problems of the Weimar Republic

Abraham, D., *The Collapse of the Weimar Republic*, Princeton, 1976
Bennett, F.W., *Germany and the Diplomacy of the Financial Crisis*, Cambridge, Mass., 1962
Brady, R., *The Rationalisation Movement in German Industry*, Berkeley, 1933
Bresciano-Turroni, C., *The Economics of Inflation*, London, 1937
Einzig, P., *Germany's Default*, London, 1934
Hardach, K., *The Political Economy of Germany in the Twentieth Century*, Berkeley, 1980
James, H., *The Reichsbank and Public Finance in Germany, 1924–1933*, Frankfurt, 1985
—, *The Great Slump in Germany*, Oxford, 1986
Kindleberger, C.P., *The World in Depression*, London, 1973
Laursen, K., and J. Pedersen, *The German Inflation, 1918–1923*, Amsterdam, 1964
Maier, C.S., *Recasting Bourgeois Europe*, Princeton, 1975
Turner, H.A., *German Big Business and Hitler*, Oxford, 1985

Politics and the Collapse of the Republic

Allen, W.S., *The Nazi Seizure of Power*, Chicago, 1965
Bessel, R., and E.J. Feuchtwanger (eds.), *Social Change and Political Development in Weimar Germany*, London, 1981
Bracher, K.D., *The German Dictatorship*, London, 1973
Carsten, F.L., *The Reichswehr and Politics*, Oxford, 1966

Dorpalen, A., *Hindenburg and the Weimar Republic*, Princeton, 1964

Eksteins, *The Limits of Reason*, London, 1975

Eyck, E., *A History of the Weimar Republic, 2 vols.*, London, 1962

Hertzman, L., *DNVP*, Lincoln, 1963

Hunt, R.N., *German Social Democracy, 1918–1933*, New Haven, 1964

Kershaw, I., *Popular Opinion and Political Dissent in the Third Reich*, Oxford, 1983

Leopold, J.A., *Alfred Hugenberg*, New Haven, 1977

Nicholls, A.J., and E. Matthias, *German Democracy and the Triumph of Hitler*, London, 1971

Stachura, P.D., *Gregor Strasser and the Rise of Nazism*, London, 1983

—, *The Nazi Machtergreifung*, London, 1983

Wheeler-Bennett, J., *The Wooden Titan*, London, 1936

Index of Names

Abegg, Otto, 101
    Wilhelm, 27
Alvensleben, Werner von, 112
Amann, Max, 60
August Wilhelm von Preußen, 99

Baden, Max von, 44
Ballerstedt, Otto, 4
Bechstein, Helene, 5
Blomberg, Gen. Werner von, 142, 145
Böss, Otto, 14
Bouhler, Philipp, 60
Boxan, —, 15
Bracher, Karl Dietrich, 93
Bracht, Franz, 119
Braun, Magnus Frhr. von, 117
    Otto, 26–30, 99, 100, 113, 121
Brecht, Arnold, 70
Breitscheid, Rudolf, 116
Briand, Aristide, 95
Briefs, Götz, 25
Bruckmann, Else, 5, 97
Brüning, Heinrich, 25, 26, 35, 80, 81,
    94–7, 99, 100, 104–17 passim, 128,
    136, 137, 147

Class, Heinrich, 74
Curtius, Julius, 106

Dahrendorf, Ralf, 39
Darré, Richard Walther, 73
Deissmann, 30
Dietrich, Marlene, 14
Dircksen, Victoria von, 98
Duesterberg, Theodor, 108, 110, 142

Ebert, Friedrich, 45, 50, 67, 80
Eckart, Dietrich, 3
    Hans von, 16, 17
Eckert, Christian, 25
Eltz-Rüberach, Paul von, 146
Esser, Hermann, 5, 53
Eyck, Erich, 70

Fallada, Hans, 72
Feder, Gottfried, 24
Fehling, Jürgen, 14
Fest, Joachim, 38
Fichte, Werner von, 60
    Johann Gottlieb, 37
Franzen, Anton, 79
Frick, Wilhelm, 4, 6, 77, 78, 97, 123,
    143
Funk, Walter, 98

Ganze, E., 15
Gayl, Wilhelm Frhr. von, 117–19,
    123, 127
Gebühr, Otto, 32
Geiger, Theodor, 87
Gessler, Otto, 8, 68
Goebbels, Joseph, 15, 18–25, 28,
    30–5, 62, 63, 79, 88, 98, 108–10,
    115, 118, 122–4, 134, 135, 137
Göring, Hermann, 5, 23, 86, 97, 98,
    121–3, 126, 138, 139, 143, 145
Graefe, Albrecht von, 53, 58
Graf, Ulrich, 5
Grauert, Ludwig, 98
Groener, Wilhelm, 50, 69, 101–3, 106,
    110–12, 114
Grzesinski, Albert, 27, 29–31, 34,
    103, 120
Gürtner, Franz, 117, 146

Hammerstein-Equord, Hans von,
    102, 141, 142, 145
Hanfstaengl, Ernst, 5, 9
Heimannsberg, Magnus, 30
Heines, Edmund, 28
Heiss, Friedrich, 8
Held, Heinrich, 58
Helfferich, Emil, 98
Helldorf, Wolf Heinrich Graf, 112,
    118
Herder, Johann Gottfried, 37
Herkner, Heinrich, 25

Index

Hess, Rudolf, 53
Hilferding, Rudolf, 80
Himmler, Heinrich, 138
Hindenburg, Paul von, 19, 26, 35,
   43, 67, 68, 80, 81, 99–103, 106–19
   passim, 123–8, 132–48
   Oskar von, 135, 136, 139, 140, 165
Hirtsiefer, Heinrich, 119
Hoffmann, Heinrich, 61
Höhler, Ali, 20
Hoover, Herbert, 95
Hugenberg, Alfred, 18, 35, 73, 74,
   76, 81, 96, 106–9, 116, 137, 138,
   142, 145, 146

Jannings, Emil, 14, 32
Jünger, Ernst, 32

Kaas, Ludwig, 115
Kahr, Gustav Ritter von, 6–9
Kalckreuth, Ebehard Count von, 137
Kaufmann, Karl, 62
Keppler, Wilhelm, 130, 131
Keudell, Walter von, 70
Killinger, Manfred von, 60
Kirdorf, Emil, 5, 97
Klagges, Dietrich, 103
Knilling, Eugen von, 7
Koch, Erich, 62
Kriebel, Hermann, 6, 7, 8, 53
Kube, Wilhelm, 28

Lagarde, Paul de, 38
Lambach, Walther, 74
Laval, Pierre, 95
Lerchenfeld, Hugo Graf von, 6, 7
Lohalm, Uwe, 43
Lohse, Hinrich, 73
Lossow, Otto von, 8, 9
Lubitsch, Ernst, 14
Ludendorff, Erich, 5, 8, 9, 44, 53, 58,
   64, 135
   Mathilde, 58
Luther, Hans, 69

Mahraun, Arthur, 25
Mann, Thomas, 30
Marx, Wilhelm, 67, 74
Maurice, Emil, 4, 53
Maurass, Charles, 38
Max, Prince von Baden, 44
Meisel, Hans, 16
Meissner, Otto, 81, 114, 134, 136,

139, 140, 144, 146
Melcher, Dr, 120
Meyer, Emil, 98
Mohler, Armin, 44
Müller, Hermann, 25, 71, 80, 81
Münchmeyer, Ludwig, 33
Mussolini, Benito, 53

Neumann, Siegmund, 66
Neurath, Constantin Frhr. von, 117,
   145
Nietzsche, Friedrich, 37

Oldenburg-Januschau, Elard von,
   135, 143

Papen, Franz von, 81, 113–19
   passim, 123–48 passim
Pfeffer, Franz von, 58–60, 87
Planck, Erwin, 117
Pol, Heinz, 32
Pöhner, Ernst, 4, 6
Pünder, Hermann, 115

Radek, Karl, 63
Rathenau, Walther, 43
Reichmann, Eva, 50
Reinhardt, Max, 14
Reinhart, Friedrich, 98
Remarque, Erich Maria, 32
Reusch, Paul, 98, 130
Ribbentrop, Joachim von, 138, 139,
   142, 143
Röhm, Ernst, 3, 58, 62, 87, 102, 112,
   124, 125, 138
Röver, Carl, 73
Rosenberg, Alfred, 53, 86
Rundstedt, Gerd von, 120

Sauckel, Fritz, 78
Schacht, Hjalmar, 75, 98, 130
Schauwecker, Franz, 32
Schemm, Hans, 85
Schiller, Friedrich, 33
Schlange-Schöningen, Hans, 116
Schleicher, Kurt von, 69, 87, 94, 101,
   102, 106, 110–14, 117, 118, 123,
   127–48 passim
Schönerer, Georg Ritter von, 38
Schröder, Kurt von, 98, 130, 132
Schwarz, Franz Xaver, 60
Schwerin von Krosigk, Lutz Graf,
   117, 145

156

Seeckt, Hans von, 8, 51, 68
Seldte, Franz, 74, 142
Severing, Carl, 27, 30, 80, 101,
    118–20
Sontheimer, Kurt, 44
Sorel, Georges, 38
Stegerwald, Adam, 116
Stempfle, Bernhard, 54
Stennes, Walter, 20–2
Stern, Fritz, 38
Strasser, Gregor, 22, 53, 58, 61–4, 88,
    107, 108, 123, 129
    Otto, 22, 62, 63, 132
Streicher, Julius, 7, 53
Stresemann, Gustav, 7, 8, 47, 52, 68,
    71, 77, 79, 80, 148

Tardieu, André, 112
Thälmann, Ernst, 68, 108, 110
Thyssen, Fritz, 98, 130

Ulrich, Curt von, 60

Vögler, Albert, 98, 130

Wagner, Josef, 62
    Richard, 5
Weber, Alfred, 25
    Christian, 5
    Friedrich, 8, 53
Weiss, Bernhard ('Isidor'), 19, 31
Wels, Otto, 116
Wessel, Horst, 16, 20
Westarp, Kuno Graf, 74, 81, 114
Wilhelm, 11, 44
Willikens, Werner, 136
Wilson, Woodrow, 44
Wirth, Joseph, 35, 106
Wissell, Rudolf, 80
Witthoeft, F. A., 98
Wolff, Theodor, 16

Zörgiebel, Karl, 14, 27–9, 31